—— Heaven's Champion ——

Heaven's Champion

William James's
Philosophy of Religion

——Ellen Kappy Suckiel——

University of Notre Dame Press
NOTRE DAME, INDIANA

Copyright 1996
by University of Notre Dame Press
Notre Dame, Indiana 46556
All Rights Reserved
Manufactured in the United States of America

Paperback 1998
ISBN 0-268-01115-X

Book design by Wendy McMillen and Jeannette Morgenroth
Set in 11/13 Galliard by Books International, Inc.

Library of Congress Cataloging-in-Publication-Data

Suckiel, Ellen Kappy.
    Heaven's champion : William James's philosophy of religion /
Ellen Kappy Suckiel.
        p.   cm.
    Includes bibliographical references and index.
    ISBN 0-268-03814-7 (alk. paper)
    1. James, William, 1842–1910—Religion.   2. Religion—
Philosophy.   3. Pragmatism.   I. Title.
    b945.j24s84   1996
    201—dc20   95-50814
                                                               CIP

For Joe,
sine quo non

It is high time to urge the use of a little imagination in philosophy.

—————William James, *Pragmatism*

Contents

Preface

At the end of the nineteenth, and the beginning of the twentieth century, William James was absorbed in thinking and writing about questions of religion. Although it is now a full century later, and there have been changes in the names of the interlocutors as well as their scholarly styles and vocabularies, the intellectual situation with regard to religion is much the same as it was in James's day. We remain challenged, by and large, by the same religious concerns, and many individuals still have doubts as to whether religious questions are even philosophically legitimate.

James believed that questions in the philosophy of religion call for a kind of imaginative response which is different from the usual approach of the academic philosopher. He thought that if we could broaden our conception of what it is to think philosophically, the issues of religion could more creatively and fruitfully be addressed. He believed that the more concretely one approached religious questions, i.e., the more one understood them in terms of the particular experiences, feelings, beliefs and actions of religious individuals, the more significant one's conclusions would be. Thus, James offered his pragmatic philosophy as a more effective and appropriate way of dealing with questions of religion. I believe that his views on this topic are fully worthy of being seriously reconsidered at this time.

This book is a critical analysis and development of James's philosophy of religion. My effort has been to integrate James's numerous writings on the topic of religion, and to show how his religious views rely upon the broader principles of his pragmatism. I have also tried to demonstrate the highly suggestive and interesting character of many of James's arguments, and of his overall approach to religious questions. In the spirit of James's appeal to concrete experience, I have utilized examples from the lives and works of scientists, composers, poets, and artists. In those arguments I have discussed which support religious belief, I have cited thinkers who are not so much theoreticians as they are genuinely religious individuals.

In writing this book, I have benefited immensely from the contribution of Joseph W. Suckiel, who has been integrally involved at every stage. His erudition and imagination, along with his philosophical and literary acuity, have enriched this work at all levels: from the earliest inception of ideas, to the structural development of the chapters, and through to the final completion of the manuscript. Besides providing moral and intellectual support, he has also kept computer hardware and software intact, and has saved the day in a number of difficult technological situations. All things considered, I like to think of this book as one outcome of our first thirty years of conversation.

I am also grateful to Professors Richard M. Gale, David L. Norton, John E. Smith, and Frank M. Oppenheim for providing astute comments at various stages of this work. I have benefited as well from several enlightening conversations about religion which I have had with David Sandler. And thanks are also due to Roberto Lint for his tireless work in securing library materials.

Finally, my work on this book has been strengthened by the example of Lilyan Kappy, my mother, a person of immeasurable resiliency and strength of purpose; and by the memory of Jack Kappy, my father, who, in his own unique way, was the first philosopher I ever knew.

This research has been generously supported by the Board of Studies in Philosophy, the Humanities Division, and the Academic Senate of the University of California, Santa Cruz.

Salinas, California
June, 1995

Abbreviations

Unless otherwise specified, the abbreviations below refer to *The Works of William James,* edited by Frederick H. Burkhardt, Fredson Bowers, and Ignas K. Skrupskelis, Cambridge: Harvard University Press.

WORKS BY JAMES

EPH *Essays in Philosophy,* 1978.
EPR *Essays in Psychical Research,* 1986.
EPS *Essays in Psychology,* 1983.
ERE *Essays in Radical Empiricism,* 1976.
ERM *Essays in Religion and Morality,* 1982.
LWJ *The Letters of William James.* Edited by Henry James. 2 vols. Boston: The Atlantic Monthly Press, 1920.
ML   *Manuscript Lectures,* 1988.
MT   *The Meaning of Truth,* 1975.
P   *Pragmatism,* 1975.
PP   *The Principles of Psychology,* 3 vols., 1981.
PU   *A Pluralistic Universe,* 1977.
SPP *Some Problems of Philosophy,* 1979.
TT   *Talks to Teachers on Psychology, and to Students on Some of Life's Ideals,* 1983.
VRE *The Varieties of Religious Experience,* 1985.
WB   *The Will to Believe,* 1979.

WORKS BY OTHERS

PPWJ   Ellen Kappy Suckiel, *The Pragmatic Philosophy of
       William James.* Notre Dame, Indiana: University
       of Notre Dame Press, 1982.
TC   Ralph Barton Perry, *The Thought and Character of
       William James.* 2 vols. Boston: Little, Brown and
       Company, 1935.

Heaven's Champion

1

Introduction

"[R]eligion is the great interest of my life," William James declared in 1897.[1] While he has come to be known among philosophers more for his pragmatic method and theory of truth than for his work on religion, there are many of James's writings—some of his most important—in which he deals with issues of religion and religious belief. Among the most prominent are "Reflex Action and Theism," "The Will to Believe," "Is Life Worth Living?," and *Human Immortality: Two Supposed Objections to the Doctrine*. Most importantly, there is James's full-length treatment of religion in *The Varieties of Religious Experience*,[2] the published version of his distinguished Gifford Lectures, delivered at Edinburgh in 1901–1902. Indeed, even many of James's works in which his main focus is elsewhere reveal his abiding interest in religious questions. In his essay "Philosophical Conceptions and Practical Results,"[3] for example, where James first introduces the pragmatic method which would become emblematic of his philosophy, he also addresses the meaning of various religious and metaphysical claims. Yet nine years later, in *Pragmatism*, when assessing the importance of "Philosophical Conceptions," James remembers religion, from among the various topics he discusses, as being the major concern of the essay (P, 29).[4] In *Pragmatism*—James's foremost statement of his pragmatic philosophy—he spends the bulk of his attention on questions of truth, meaning, and philosophical methodology. Yet he

3

deals with these issues not solely for their own intellectual interest and importance, but also because he recognizes that his conclusions about them help solve questions about the significance and justification of religious belief. Lecture VIII of *Pragmatism* is devoted specifically to the question of pragmatism and religion, and Lectures II and III contain significant discussions of religious matters as well. James's writings on psychical research are also significant for his views on religion. For one of James's aims in these writings is to extend the domain of what might count as possible evidence for the truth of religious claims. He believes that a rigorous assessment of psychical experiences might provide evidence against materialistic and mechanistic models of causality, and thereby open the way to a more open-minded assessment of the veridicality of religious experience (EPR, 134). *A Pluralistic Universe* is yet another of James's works having significance for his philosophy of religion. In this work he develops a metaphysical basis for his conception of God, and outlines the religious implications of his metaphysical views.[5]

In James's personal life, he expressed a certain degree of ambivalence toward religion. In response to a questionnaire in 1904, James made several interesting remarks. He reported that God was only "dimly" real to him, and that he had never experienced God's presence (LWJ, 2:213–14). In a letter to James Leuba that same year, James wrote that he had "no living sense of commerce with a God," but he also went on to add that there was something in him—a "mystical germ"—which responded when he heard religious utterances made by others (LWJ, 2:211). His report merely that he was sympathetic to the religious claims of others appears to under-represent the full range of James's religious sensibilities, however, since in other contexts he reports having experiences which, although not of a full-blown mystical character, are clearly religious in nature.[6]

To the question "Do you believe in personal immortality?" James replied, "Never keenly" (LWJ, 2:214). He also admitted, however, that he believed in immortality more strongly as he grew older. His reason: "Because I am just getting fit to live" (LWJ, 2:214). In response to a further question as to whether he prayed, James reported that he could not possibly pray, because it made him feel "foolish and artificial" (LWJ, 2:214). He also asserted that he had "grown so out of Christianity," that in order for him to appreciate other people's reports of their religious experiences, any Christian doctrinal elements of those reports would have to be "abstracted from and overcome" (LWJ, 2:211).[7] On the other hand, in spite of these remarks about Christianity and prayer, James, while on the Harvard campus, is reported to have stopped every day at the church in Harvard Yard.[8]

Whatever his ambivalence, one thing is clear: James was exercised deeply by religious questions, and he devoted his talents both as a psychologist and as a philosopher to their resolution.

A central principle of James's philosophy of religion is that questions of religious truth and the justification of religious belief must be approached from the proper perspective in order to be answered satisfactorily. The point of his work in the philosophy of religion is, first, to eliminate those approaches which impede progress in understanding and assessing religious claims; and second, to develop an enriched and more sensitive set of criteria by which such progress may be achieved.

In Lecture I of *Pragmatism*, the book in which James most fully articulates his philosophical methodology, he announces that the chief purpose of his pragmatic philosophy is to mediate between traditional philosophical dualisms which have shown themselves to be intractably at loggerheads.[9] James asserts that "the present dilemma in philosophy," as it relates to the topic of religion, is as follows: On the one hand, there are the empirical, typically scientifically-oriented philosophers, who retain high standards of rigor in requiring that beliefs be justified by empirical evidence. Given their conception of the nature of empirical evidence and their commitment to conventional standards of scientific reasoning, these philosophers feel forced to reject religious claims. On the other hand, there are the speculative philosophers, particularly the absolute idealists and transcendentalists. These philosophers retain a perspective which may be called religious, but James thinks it is one which is so thoroughly abstract and empirically empty that it is irrelevant to the lives of religious believers.

One key objection that James has to the speculative philosophers is that these thinkers see religious questions as essentially theoretical ones, resolvable exclusively by intellectual argument. The notion that it is suitable to look for the justification of religious belief on intellectual or theoretical grounds is, of course, a long-standing and venerable one. But it is also problematic when viewed from a personal perspective. For individuals who hold religious beliefs usually do not do so on the basis of argument; and it is unlikely that any argument taken by itself would convince anyone to believe, who was not already personally disposed to accept the religious point of view. Moreover, it is unlikely that religious individuals would renounce their beliefs on the basis of any argument against religion, even if it appeared conclusive. But if, in many cases, a person's religious beliefs are not held exclusively, or even primarily, on the basis of rational argument, we might justifiably wonder whether intellectual reasoning misses the point (or at least a great deal of the point) in regard to religion.[10]

James thinks that those philosophers who succumb to the temptation to see religious issues as intellectual or theoretical ones do so because they divorce themselves from the really significant aspects of religion, namely, the concrete feelings and experiences of religious believers. Indeed, rather than elevate religious discourse, James thinks that rational argumentation desiccates and trivializes it.[11] James's philosophy of religion is founded on his belief that feeling and experience are the profounder sources of religious truth. As he was preparing the Gifford Lectures, in a letter to a friend, James expressed his primary aim, which was this:

> [T]o defend . . . "experience" against "philosophy" as being the real backbone of the world's religious life—I mean prayer, guidance, and all that sort of thing immediately and privately felt, as against high and noble general views of our destiny and the world's meaning. . . . (LWJ, 2:127)[12]

As James rejects intellectualizing and theorizing about religion in favor of an empirical approach, his task becomes that of articulating the way in which experience may justify religious beliefs. While James thinks that the topic of religion should be approached empirically, he realizes that this approach, particularly in the hands of scientistic thinkers, often results in the rejection of religious claims.

James's use of an empiricist methodology to support, rather than reject religion is especially noteworthy when seen in light of his historical context. The larger cultural mileau in which James lived was profoundly scientistic. Materialism, positivism, and agnosticism were among the dominant intellectual positions of the day, and the prevailing ideology was that scientific reasoning is appropriate to all areas of intellectual discourse, including morality and religion.[13] While James ultimately was ambivalent about the relationship between science and religion, as we shall see in chapter 7, of one thing he felt certain: to use the authority of science in support of "agnostic positivism" (WB, 50) or "crude naturalism" (P, 144) is a profound mistake.

I shall use the term "scientific rationalist" to refer to those thinkers who repudiate the claims of religion on the basis of particular views about the ways in which beliefs may be justified. Scientific rationalists do not always explicitly articulate their position. But even when they do not, they may be recognized by the attitude with which they approach metaphysical and epistemological issues in general, and religious issues in particular. We may get a clearer idea of their position by examining a cluster of beliefs to which they are characteristically committed.

Scientific rationalists think that scientific reasoning stands as the paradigm of rational discourse. They believe that claims about matters of fact, including putative religious facts, can be justified only on the basis of what they regard as scientifically acceptable empirical evidence. In addition, they hold that since religious experiences, feelings, and intuitions are personal and subjective, they are thereby lacking in evidentiary significance. Thus scientific rationalists reject, as unjustified, religious claims which are based on the appeal to any such subjective phenomena.

Scientific rationalists also reject pragmatic arguments in support of religious claims. Since pragmatic arguments in support of beliefs provide reasons which are consequentialist rather than evidentiary in nature, they are considered irrelevant to those beliefs' justification.

Further, scientific rationalists consider the supernatural postulations of religion to be unscientific, insofar as they do not refer to processes or objects in the natural world. They hold that such postulations are unworthy of belief, or even of serious consideration.[14] In contrast to religious thinkers, scientific rationalists are inclined to offer naturalistic and reductionistic accounts of the genesis of religious beliefs. They regard belief in God as having no genuine reference to a divine reality; for they hold that such belief is fully explicable in terms of the believer's physiological, psychological, or social conditions, motives, or needs. Proffering these reductionistic explanations of the causes of religious beliefs, scientific rationalists are inclined to regard themselves (albeit illogically) as having obviated any reason we might have to consider those beliefs to be true.[15]

In light of their intellectual commitments, scientific rationalists find it easy to reject religious claims; but a deeper approach to the issues of religion will reveal that their perspective is unnecessarily exclusionary. Scientific rationalists exhibit a bias, or prejudice, in that they consider questions to be closed which legitimately may be regarded as open. As we shall see below, James believes that scientific rationalists display both an overly narrow conception of what may count as scientific evidence, as well as an overly broad conception of the legitimate domain of science. He thinks that they beg the question against religion, by disallowing, in advance, the possibility of the kinds of conclusions that richer conceptions of justification and evidence would permit.

Although they view themselves as open-minded and rational, scientific rationalists often maintain their position with an unusual level of self-assurance and complacency, at times even arrogance, adopting a condescending stance toward religious believers. Typical of the scientific rationalists to whom James objects are W. K. Clifford and Thomas Huxley (WB, 17–18, 77–78). But scientific rationalism is as influential a philosophical standpoint in our own day as it was in James's. The following statements, illustrating the tenor of this position, span the period between James's time and our own.

W. V. O. Quine, for example, makes the following claim:

> [D]o we know that theism is false? . . . Science . . . is open always to correction by further scientific advances, *but there are no alternative avenues of discovery*. Barring one or another inordinate reinterpretation of terms, it can be affirmed with all the confidence of sound scientific judgment that there is no God or afterlife.[16]

In *Moses and Monotheism,* Sigmund Freud has this to say about religious belief:

> How we who have little belief envy those who are convinced of the existence of a Supreme Power, for whom the world holds no problems. . . . How comprehensive, exhaustive and final are the doctrines of the believers compared with the laboured, poor and patchy attempts at explanation which are the best we can produce. . . . We can only regret it if certain experiences of life and observations of nature have made it impossible to accept the hypothesis of such a Supreme Being. As if the world had not enough problems, we are confronted with the task to find out how those who have faith in a Divine Being could have acquired it, and whence this belief derives the enormous power that enables it to overwhelm Reason and Science.[17]

And finally, consider this claim by Bertrand Russell:

> God and immortality, the central dogmas of the Christian religion, find no support in science. . . . I cannot see any ground for either. I do not pretend to be able to prove that there is no God. I equally cannot prove that Satan is a fiction. The Christian God may exist; so may the Gods of Olympus, or of ancient Egypt, or of Babylon. But no one of these hypotheses is more probable than any other: they lie outside the region of even probable knowledge, and therefore there is no reason to consider any of them.[18]

As I have noted, James shares with the scientific rationalists a commitment to an empirical approach to religion. But he also believes, in opposition to them, that a sufficiently thorough examination of religion, conjoined with a more insightful understanding of the criteria by which it should be judged, will support, rather than undermine, religious conclusions. "Let empiricism once become associated with religion," James claims, "as hitherto . . . it has been associated with irreligion, and . . . a new era of religion as well as of philosophy will be ready to begin" (PU, 142).

James offers the following definition of religion in *Varieties*, in order to circumscribe the focus of his concern. He is interested in neither the speculative theories of the philosophers and theologians, nor in institutionalized religion, which he sees as just a social or political phenomenon. He is interested in religion only as it is understood in personal terms:

> Religion . . . shall mean for us the feelings, acts, and experiences of individual men in their solitude, so far as they apprehend themselves to stand in relation to whatever they may consider the divine. (VRE, 34)[19]

The meaning and importance of James's religious writings can properly be understood only in the light of his belief that the most fruitful approach to religion is an empirical one. *Varieties*, in particular, represents the consummate expression of James's empirical approach. It is largely devoted to numerous, detailed descriptions of religious experiences. Almost a century after its publication, it is still widely regarded as unrivaled in the religious literature as a monument of descriptive psychology. And this assessment is correct. But to see *Varieties*, as many do, as *just*, or even primarily, a descriptive work, is to fail to appreciate its true significance.[20] However brilliant it is as a study in the psychology of religion, in fact James's descriptions of religious experience in this book are provided to support a program which is most definitely and deeply philosophical. As it would be misleading and counterproductive to do art, music, or literary criticism without due attention to the concrete practices and products of artists, musicians, and writers, James believes it would be equally misleading to think philosophically about religion without due regard for concrete experiences, feelings, beliefs, and desires of religious individuals. Indeed, James's emphasis on concrete cases in *Varieties* mirrors his more general belief about the relevance of empirical facts to philosophy, as can be seen in his wry remarks in "The Teaching of Philosophy in Our Colleges":

"G. S. H." speaks of the "application of philosophical systems to history, politics and law." We hope he does not mean that these should be taught separately from the ordinary historical, political and legal courses. That would be building a house and getting a man from the city to come down and put on the "architecture" afterwards. (EPH, 5)[21]

In his writings on religion, James immerses himself and his readers in detailed descriptions of religious feeling, experience, and the circumstances of religious belief. Like turning the facets of a cut stone under the light, illuminating them one by one, James illuminates the diverse ways in which religious beliefs may be justified. On the one hand, he argues against the speculative philosophers and theologians, by showing the limits of intellectual discourse in religion, and by defending the possibility of preconceptual knowledge of the divine. On the other hand, he argues that the agnosticism of the scientific rationalist is predicated upon an excessively narrow and unimaginative understanding of what may count as evidence for religious claims, and the ways in which that evidence may be utilized. James seeks to show that there is evidence in abundance for the truth of religious belief, once one knows how to recognize and use it; and that it is no defect of religious apprehensions that those who do not acknowledge this evidence are unable to see beyond the narrow limits which they themselves have imposed on the situation.

In addition to evidential justifications for religious belief, James develops pragmatic arguments as well. If religious beliefs lead to good consequences in the subject's life, James contends, then these constitute *prima facie* reasons for holding them. James does not expect the scientific rationalists to be sympathetic to his pragmatic arguments for religion. But, as we shall see, he does feel that they have rendered themselves incapable of even understanding what might be at stake, pragmatically, in holding religious beliefs. James argues that because the scientific rationalists close themselves off to significant philosophical possibilities, their belief policies are both unimaginative and self-defeating.

James's pragmatic justification for religious belief often has been challenged, on both epistemic and moral grounds. From an epistemic standpoint, critics have argued that James's accounts of religious truth and the justification of religious belief are perniciously subjectivistic. As we shall see, however, once James's conceptions of religious truth and justification are understood in their full measure of depth, this charge may be dismissed.

The moral objections to James's philosophy of religion have been no less severe than the epistemic ones. James's pragmatic justification for religious belief is thought to be a disguised form of humanism, a support of religious belief made solely by appeal to the beneficial consequences in the life of the believer which follow upon religious commitment. James's defense of religion is regarded as an appeal to narrow self-interest, and as such, it is considered to be fundamentally incongruous with the elevated domain of religious concerns. But in fact, James holds that the most significant pragmatic consequences of religious belief do not involve the believer's narrow, personal benefit. Rather they involve a set of consequences which are highly idealized. For James contends that our deepest moral responsibilities, as well as opportunities, may be appreciated only when our lives are understood in religious terms. As we shall see, James bases his views of the meaning and moral significance of religious belief upon a set of metaphysical claims about

the moral perfectibility of the world, and human beings'
proper place in that context.

My aim in this book is to demonstrate the credibility and
power of James's philosophy of religion, and to examine
the moral, epistemic, and metaphysical implications of his
views. My intention is to interpret and develop James's philosophy of religion in a way that enables his views to be
understood and appraised with the subtlety and sophisti-
cation which I believe are appropriate to them, but which
too often have been denied them. On the one hand, James
tends to be dismissive of the speculative philosopher's approach to religion.[22] On the other hand, he shares a commitment to empiricism with the scientific rationalist. Thus,
he finds the scientific rationalist to be a far more provocative
and formidable philosophical adversary. In this book, I shall
concentrate on showing the effectiveness of James's answer
to the scientific rationalist, though a number of arguments
will be applicable to the speculative philosopher as well. As
I shall show, James is not satisfied just to defend religion
against scientific rationalist objections. He also takes the of-
fensive and tries to demonstrate the ways in which scientific
rationalism fails as a philosophical position.

As we shall see in the chapters which follow, in some
of James's discussions, he focuses on what he regards as the
preconceptual character of certain forms of religious knowledge. Elsewhere, in emphasizing the interpretive character
of certain religious claims, he focuses on the religious individual's reliance upon conceptual thought. And while on
some occasions James argues that religious beliefs may be
justified on pragmatic grounds, on other occasions he contends that they must be capable of empirical confirmation.
While all of his analyses share the common characteristic
of approaching religion from the viewpoint of experience,
broadly conceived, it would be a mistake to look to James
for a single, coherent theory of the justification of religious

belief. For his aim was neither to develop such a theory, nor to establish, conclusively, that God exists, or that any other particular religious claims are true. Following out his pragmatic and empiricist program, James's aim was to help his readers see new ways of approaching the questions of religion, and to open the debate to a more judicious and imaginative assessment of the possibilities. To this end, James examined various philosophical impediments to religious belief, in order to undermine their persuasiveness and authority. His aim was to show, piece by piece and one by one, from an epistemic point of view, how the field is open to the genuine possibility of God's existence, and how one may justifiably believe in God if one so chooses.[23] James thought it sufficient to show how, by retaining a probabilistic, hypothetical, and open-minded stance, we may make intelligent judgments in favor of religious claims. On the basis of our acknowledgement of these epistemic possibilities, moreover, James sought to show how we may better appreciate and actualize the significant moral possibilities which, he believed, only the religious point of view can generate and sustain. This was James's program in religion and in this he shows remarkable consistency and insight.

A study of James's philosophy of religion is valuable not only for its own intrinsic interest, but also because it reveals a great deal about his more general philosophical positions. The topic of religion provides James with an opportunity for working through a set of related issues which were of deep and abiding concern to him. Among these are questions regarding the epistemic priority of experience and feeling, the role of faith in the justification of belief, the nature of religious truth, and the limits of philosophic rationality. These issues will be illuminated as our discussion proceeds.

2

The Challenge to Religion

In this chapter, we shall look at what it means to see the world in religious terms, and demonstrate some of the ways in which religious beliefs may be defended against objections. James offers an analysis of religious belief which, I shall argue, is more sensitive to the meaning of religious claims than is that of the scientific rationalist. He also offers a more comprehensive and subtle account of the ways in which religious claims may be justified.

I

A religious understanding of the world enables believers to see the superficial, prosaic facts of their lives in a context of deeper significance: if God exists, our lives gain meaning in relation to that divine reality. To better appreciate what is involved in seeing the world from a religious point of view, it will be helpful to compare how markedly individuals may differ in their fundamental philosophical and emotional responses to the question of the significance of human life, depending on whether their outlook is secular or religious.

Secular thinkers, typically scientific rationalists, are inclined to hold either that life has no meaning at all, or that it has only the meaning we ascribe to it. Among the many thinkers who have taken this position, several examples are particularly illustrative. Sigmund Freud, for instance, is

resolutely dismissive of the desire to understand life's meaning. He holds that concern about the meaning of life is
just a symptom of psychological ill-health. "The moment a
man questions the meaning and value of life," Freud claims,
"he is sick, since objectively neither has any existence."[1]
Albert Camus provides another illuminating example. In
his well-known essay, "The Myth of Sisyphus," Camus takes
that myth to be illustrative of the meaning of life. As Sisyphus is prisoner to the arduous, eternal, and unredeemed
task of rolling a large rock up to the top of a mountain—
only, time after time, to have it roll down again; so also,
Camus thinks, are human beings engaged in the fundamentally futile activities of which their lives are constituted.[2]

Some Anglo-American philosophers are no more sanguine about life's deeper meaning. R. M. Hare joins other
more recent philosophers in offering a linguistic analysis
of the meaning of life. He claims that it is a misuse of language to ask whether anything objectively matters. He argues
that "when we say something matters or is important what
we are doing, in saying this, is to express concern about
that something."[3] We are not indicating any objective fact
about that thing itself. On Hare's view, while it makes
perfectly good sense to claim that one's life matters *to oneself*, one would not be justified in claiming that it matters
simpliciter—viz., that it has genuine meaning independent
of one's preferences and desires.

Finally, much like Camus, Thomas Nagel holds that life is
absurd.[4] He characterizes an absurd situation as one which
"includes a conspicuous discrepancy between pretension or
aspiration and reality."[5] He playfully likens the absurdity of
life as a whole to more mundane absurd circumstances: "a
notorious criminal is made president of a major philan-
thropic foundation," for example, or "you declare your love
over the telephone to a recorded announcement."[6] Human
life is absurd, Nagel believes, because while we approach our

lives with the utmost seriousness, we can also see that, from a deeper perspective, our own seriousness seems gratuitous and everything to which we are committed seems arbitrary.[7]

If the views just cited are any indication of the resources secular thinkers have available to deal with questions concerning life's meaning, it is hardly surprising that religious individuals consider the secular perspective woefully inadequate. For from the religious perspective, these secular thinkers will be thought merely to dismiss the significant questions, rather than attempt to answer them. Whatever differences there may be among particular religious doctrines, a characteristic quality of religious consciousness is the sense that each particular item in existence is, at least ultimately, an expression, creation, or manifestation of a divine reality. The divine reality may be regarded as a personal creator (as in Judeo-Christian religions), or a principle of oneness (as in transcendentalism and certain forms of Hinduism and Buddhism). It may even be regarded as a principle of mathematical coherency or a form of scientific mystery— views at the limit of the concept of the religious which are not uncommonly held by physicists.[8] James's own view, as we shall see, is that the divine reality is the widest possible field of consciousness, of which our own more limited consciousness is just a part. The issue of importance for us, however, is not the varying specific theological doctrines to which different religious believers are committed, but rather the underlying sense of a divine reality (however broadly understood) which all (or most all) of them share.[9]

James holds that religious believers regard themselves as perceiving "a supersensuous meaning to the ordinary outward data of consciousness" (VRE, 338); they come "naturally to think that the smallest details of this world derive infinite significance from their relation to an unseen divine order" (VRE, 294). As we shall see, it is a question of considerable complexity as to precisely what James counts as a meaningful religious claim. In whatever way that ultimately may be analyzed, however, one thing is clear: James often emphasizes that religious claims are not about ordinary empirical facts *simpliciter*. Rather (as is testified by the title of Lecture III of *Varieties*, "The Reality of the Unseen"), they are claims about the deeper spiritual reality which is thought to underlie those facts. James describes the way in which the believer interprets everyday experience as having religious significance:

> When we see all things in God, and refer all things to him, we read in common matters superior expressions of meaning. The deadness with which custom invests the familiar vanishes, and existence as a whole appears transfigured. (VRE, 375)

James makes the point again, as follows. For the religious individual:

> The outward face of nature need not alter, but the expressions of meaning in it alter. It was dead and is alive again. It is like the difference between looking on a person without love, or upon the same person with love. (VRE, 373)[10]

One way to express James's position is to say that the most striking difference between the religious believer and the non-believer is the former's sense of the supernal nature of existence. The experience of some religious individuals may take dramatic form. For example, to imagine an individual fully engaged in the reverent and awe-inspiring awareness of God—as Rudolph Otto would put it, the "mysterium tremendum et fascinans"[11]—is to imagine a situation of the most intense possible gravity, profundity, and significance. But equally noteworthy are those who see such religious meaning in the more ordinary facts of everyday life. These individuals articulate the qualities of religious consciousness which James describes. They believe that all things, including human beings, have a meaningful place in the context of a more profound reality. It is notable that poets are among the best representatives of the religious point of view. William Blake, for example, enjoins us:

> To see a World in a Grain of Sand
> And a Heaven in a Wild Flower[12]

Gerard Manley Hopkins concurs, if more dramatically, when he proclaims:

> The world is charged with the grandeur of God.
> It will flame out, like shining from shook foil.[13]

Simone Weil, French mystic and philosopher, in her essay "Love of the Order of the World," echoes sentiments similar to Hopkins's, specifically as they relate to the question of the meaning of human life. In the following passage, she identifies a religious dimension in seemingly prosaic and ordinary events:

> [I]n every kind of human occupation there is always some regard for the beauty of the world seen in more or less distorted or soiled images. As a consequence there is not any department of human life which is purely natural. The supernatural is secretly present throughout. Under a thousand different forms, grace and mortal sin are everywhere.[14]

Finally, Thomas Merton—poet, writer, Catholic monk— also expresses the view that even the most mundane contexts of life embody religious significance. Merton describes the religious sensibility of a couple he knew:

> [T]hey were certainly saints. . . . sanctified by leading ordinary lives in a completely supernatural manner, sanctified by obscurity, by usual skills, by common tasks, by routine, but skills, tasks, routine which received a supernatural form from grace within, and from the habitual union of their souls with God in deep faith and charity.[15]

The scientific rationalist is likely to dismiss claims such as these, arguing that rather than describing the facts per se, the religious believer offers only a personal and unsupportable interpretation of them. The scientific rationalist may grant that a religious understanding of the world can fulfill the believer's desire for a sense of deeper meaning, and provide a certain kind of psychological security. But such personal satisfactions, it may be argued, are not sufficient to support the claim that religious interpretations of the world are justified, much less true. The scientific rationalist is likely to claim, for instance, that regarding Thomas Merton's description of his friends, the actual facts are no more than that the people to whom he refers fulfilled the mundane tasks of their daily lives. The attribution of deeper meaning to their activities, and the belief that their tasks are sanctified, are purely emotional interpretations on Merton's part. Nothing whatever about the existence of God may be inferred from his beliefs.

Similarly in the case of the claim made by Weil. In the passage we have cited, she asserts that beauty appears in distorted or soiled images. But, the scientific rationalist may ask, would it not be simpler and more rational, in cases where Weil says that beauty is hidden by the distortion of its embodiment, to say simply that beauty does not appear at all? What difference would it make perceptually if the latter claim were chosen rather than the former? Why should Weil's, or Merton's, way of seeing things be considered anything more than an unnecessarily complicated interpretation of their experience, subjective and sentimental, unsupported by the simple facts at hand? Why should they not be seen as gratuitously enhancing their experience by appeal to an added layer of meaning, and by reference to a superfluous metaphysical entity?

Because the scientific view of the world purportedly represents (or at least more closely represents) the strictly observable facts as they present themselves, some may conclude that it is the scientific rationalist, rather than the religious believer, who occupies the logical high ground. But is this true? The fact that religious beliefs may involve interpretations of strictly observable empirical facts is not enough—at least not enough by itself—to obviate the possibility of their objective pertinence.[16] While there is no doubt that *some* interpretive claims are clearly personal and idiosyncratic, there is no reason to assume that they *all* are. Why accept what seems to be the scientific rationalist's assumption that the more narrow the criterion one uses to identify a fact, the more closely one refers to directly observable appearances, the closer one's description will be to the truth?

To better appreciate this point, it may help to reflect upon non-religious contexts, and see how much interpretation we commonly allow, without objection, in understanding objects and events as having deeper meaning. The area of ethics provides a rich source of examples. In one instance, a Polish Jewish survivor of the Holocaust was recently interviewed about the years of his childhood in which he was hidden from the Nazis in the basement of a Polish Catholic woman. In grateful tears, the man proclaimed that this woman and the other Poles who had hidden Jews had "saved the honor of Poland." Many of us would accept the truth of his assertion, indeed, welcome it as recording one of the striking manifestations of human goodness in an otherwise tragic period.

The survivor's claim, of course, is a highly interpretive one, reaching beneath the benefactors' actions to a deeper level of meaning. The claim that this woman helped save the honor of Poland registers a more profound observation than the claim merely that she hid the child. While the deeper claim may be more controversial, it would be obtuse to assert that it is somehow suspect in principle, on the sole ground that it registers a profounder and less immediately obvious fact.

But if it is appropriate to understand actions in terms of upholding the honor of a country, why should it be thought so much more dubious to interpret actions in terms of religious characteristics such as that of being "holy" or "sanctified"? It might be suggested that the difference between ethical claims such as those about honor, on the one hand, and typical religious claims, on the other, is that the former do not presuppose a set of non-empirically determinable metaphysical commitments, while (with some exceptions) the latter surely do. Particularly in the case of Judeo-Christian religions, religious attributions of "sanctity," and the like, are built upon a foundation of belief in the existence of a supernatural being.

But are religious judgments really significantly different from ethical judgments in the kinds of beliefs they presuppose? A moment's reflection will show that the history of ethics chronicles an attempt to discover the foundation of ethical value, in terms of which the meaning of our ethical judgments may properly be understood. But except for naturalistic ethical theories, claims describing such foundations are like religious claims in that they involve reliance upon non-empirically determinable metaphysical commitments.[17] These include, to name a few, the Forms in Plato's ethical philosophy, noumenal freedom as the basis for the categorical imperative in Kant's, and goodness as a non-natural property in the ethical philosophy of G. E. Moore. Even attempts at naturalistic ethical theories, designed specifically to escape what is regarded to be the problem of positing transcendental bases for ethical value, are not always immune from non-empirically determinable foundations. John Stuart Mill's eudaimonism, for instance, does not rely exclusively on empirically describable pleasures and pains, as he sometimes avows, but rather on an idealized conception of human nature embedded in his normative conception of happiness.[18]

It is important to note, however, that whatever philosophical problems there might be in articulating a non-empirically determinable foundation of moral value, this does not prevent us from making everyday moral judgments. Indeed, we probably could not stop if we tried. While one may be a stalwart relativist, nihilist, or sceptic theoretically, it may also be the case, as Bernard Williams has suggested, that only a psychopathic individual could utterly abrogate all moral judgments in his or her practical life.[19] Whatever difficulties we may have in articulating their theoretical foundations, we do not call into question the fact that we have moral sensibilities, which, in a general way, we feel we are entitled to trust.

But if moral sensibilities may be trusted, in spite of whatever theoretical problems they may engender, why should religious and spiritual sensibilities be more cursorily dismissed? Whatever the differences between the distinct theologies, and whatever their logical or theoretical problems, no questions on the level of metaphysical commitment by themselves are sufficient to impugn the belief of religious individuals that they are apprehending a spiritual dimension of reality.

Of course, as questions endure regarding the foundation of ethics, deep and pervasive questions in religion also remain. For James's part, as we shall see, he aims to construct a philosophy of religion which involves a minimal degree of metaphysical commitment. He does this in order to retain as close as possible a connection to the solid evidence for religion which is provided by the religious individual's fundamental sense of a divine reality, independent of any potentially more problematic intellectual doctrines with which it might be associated.

The more general point at stake in this discussion concerns the extent to which any interpretive claims—ethical, religious, or others—may be considered justifiable. For if interpretive claims are not justifiable, then insofar as James treats religious beliefs as interpretations of empirical facts, they would be consigned to a merely subjective and personal status.[20] While it is certainly true that some interpretive claims may not be justified, I have tried to show that it would be short-sighted to reject, *tout court*, any interpretation which purports to penetrate beyond the obvious facts of directly perceived experience. From the religious perspective, the religious sceptic is like a person who listens to Beethoven's Fifth Symphony and hears the notes but not the melodic themes, or hears the melodies but fails to discern the symphony's grandeur and loftiness.[21] The sceptic is like the individual who interprets Michelangelo's Florence Pietà, executed very late in his life and intended for his own tomb, in terms exclusively of line, form, or other compositional elements, but fails to discern (as one critic has described it) the expression of "suffering, death, and redemption" in the work.[22] Some properties cannot be disclosed by the simplest level of descriptive observation terms.[23] Indeed, it is precisely this fact which leads us to honor the most sensitive and discerning among us for being able to recognize them.[24]

Returning specifically to the scientific rationalist's challenge to religion, we may conclude that when Weil says that beauty appears in distorted and soiled images, it would make no point against her to claim that on scientific rationalist principles, we would be unable to discern this. Under the constraints of scientific rationalism, there would be no reason to expect that we could. Paradoxically, under the guise of preserving objectivity, the scientific rationalist declines to use the very mechanisms of sensibility and understanding by which religious facts, if they are genuine, are capable of being recognized. Thus, unless one could establish on independent grounds that non-religious ways of perceiving the world were the most accurate ones (and what could such grounds be, which did not beg the question?), there would be no reason to deny the objectivity of religious belief on the basis of those who fail to perceive the world in religious terms. I shall not here take up the complex and difficult challenge of developing criteria for distinguishing between profound judgments on the one hand and merely sentimental, personal, or mistaken interpretations on the other. While it is, of course, essential to have such standards, and while religious claims may require some unique standards of their own, there is still no reason, at the outset, to think that religion is more in need of these standards than many other significant areas of belief.

II

As we have just seen, the scientific rationalist has no warrant for claiming that religious interpretations of the world are merely subjective. With this point established, let us now turn our attention to one important argument which James offers to justify religious belief. For the remainder of this chapter, we shall consider the central argument of "The Will to Believe," an essay in which James specifically addresses the challenge of religious scepticism, and which includes his best-known attempt to justify religious belief on pragmatic grounds. As we shall see, in this essay James provides not only a pragmatic justification for religious belief, but he also uses his pragmatic argument to highlight further the deficiencies of the scientific rationalist position.

The central concept in "The Will to Believe," and the one which has received the most attention, is the notion of a "genuine option." James defines a "genuine option" as a choice between alternative beliefs which is "live," "forced," and "momentous" (WB, 14). It will be helpful to clarify what he means by these terms. A live option, according to

James, is constituted by alternative hypotheses that are themselves both "live" (as opposed to "dead"), and by this James
means that each hypothesis appeals to the subject as being
within the range of possible beliefs a person might hold.
The liveness of an option for an individual is largely an emotional matter—in James's vivid language, in a live option,
each hypothesis makes an "electric connection" with the
subject's nature (WB, 14). Most present-day readers, for example would not find the option "Be a Heraclitean or be a
Parmenidean" to be a live one. To be live, an option must
be pertinent to the individual's life. An option is "forced,"
according to James, when the subject *must* choose one of
the available alternatives. "Every dilemma based on a complete logical disjunction," he claims, "with no possibility of
not choosing, is an option of this forced kind" (WB, 15). In
the case of religion, the forced option is either to accept or
refuse to accept the claim that God exists. Finally, James calls
an option "momentous" if it meets three additional criteria:
the option must be one in which the opportunity to choose
is unique, the stakes must be significant, and the decision
must be irreversible (WB, 15).

Let us look first at James's notion of a forced option, for
his use of this concept in the religious context might seem
problematic. Why would James hold that there is no third
alternative between believing that God exists on the one
hand, and rejecting the claim that He exists on the other?
Why would he want to abrogate what seems to be the
perfectly functional three-part distinction between belief,
disbelief, and the withholding of judgment? James's view
seems clearly to fly in the face of the fact that a large number of people consider themselves, without any sense of
logical difficulty, to be agnostics.

The apparent peculiarity of James's position is dissipated, however, once we appreciate his deeper agenda. If
the question of whether to believe in God were an exclu-

sively intellectual one, James grants that it would be possible to withhold judgment. But he believes that agnosticism, while *theoretically* a distinct alternative, is, from a *pragmatic* perspective, in terms of the concrete role religious belief plays in the individual's life, no different from atheism. The important fact, James believes, is that atheism and agnosticism are both alike in being choices to decline to believe in God. From a pragmatic perspective, it is irrelevant whether the rejection of religious belief occurs through the atheist's denial or the agnostic's non-commitment. This is so, James argues, because *if* God exists, then both the agnostic and the atheist, in declining to believe, lose the benefits of religious belief, as well as the knowledge of their appropriate religious responsibilities (WB, 31).[25] We should note in passing that the use of the notion of a "forced option" allows James to make an interesting point about all forms of scepticism; namely, that a person can withhold belief and thus maintain neutrality only in matters where no important stakes are involved. In cases where the consequences in the believer's life of withholding belief are the same as those which occur from actually denying belief, then from a *pragmatic* perspective, neutrality is impossible.

Let us now consider what James means when he claims that the choice to believe in God is a "momentous" option. As we have indicated, James defines the concept of a "momentous" option in terms of three further characteristics. For an option to be momentous, the opportunity to choose must be "unique," the decision "irreversible," and the stakes "significant." Looking at the condition that the stakes be significant, it is clear that the choice to believe in God is profoundly significant. For as we have seen in section I, religious believers are able to understand their lives as grounded in divine meaning, and thus have reassurance that they have an integral and fitting place in the world order. Moreover, according to James (as we shall see more fully

in chapter 6), their belief provides them with reason and
motivation to reach toward an ideal of moral and spiritual
perfection which is unavailable to non-believers.

But does the choice to believe in God also meet James's
other necessary conditions of a momentous option—that of
being unique and irreversible? I suggest that in the context
of religion, the concepts of irreversibility and uniqueness
require broad interpretation. For it would be odd if James
meant to suggest that the option to believe in God were
unique or irreversible at any single point in a person's life.
Unlike an example he gives in "The Will to Believe," of a
choice to decide on a once-in-a-lifetime opportunity to join
a polar expedition (WB, 15), decisions about whether to
believe in God are typically reversible. Indeed, many individuals struggling with the question of God's existence can
testify to this fact. Moreover, regarding the condition that
the choice to believe in God be unique, it would be most
unusual for there to be a single, irreplaceable opportunity in
the course of an individual's life to choose religious belief.
With the exception of figures like St. Paul on the road to
Damascus, most individuals make their religious decisions in
more ordinary and repeatable contexts.[26]

Is James wrong, then, to speak of the irreversibility and
uniqueness of the choice to adopt religious belief? I do not
think so. Although he has not made his intention as clear as
he might have, I think that James has in mind a broader perspective within which to understand the choice to believe.
"We have but this one life," he claims, "in which to take up
our attitude" toward metaphysical and religious issues (SPP,
115). If one views one's existence not as a series of discrete
choice points, but rather in terms of one's life as a whole,
then the choice whether to configure one's life in religious
terms is understandably unique and irreversible.[27] When understood in this broader context, one's choice either to live
or not live a life which is integrated with religious commit-

ment is significant, unique, and irreversible: it meets all of James's conditions for being a momentous option.

James uses the distinctions he draws in "The Will to Believe" to justify religious belief on pragmatic grounds. He argues that the choice to believe in God is forced and momentous. Moreover, there are no adequate intellectual grounds upon which the choice can be made. Given these conditions, if the subject also regards the choice to believe as live, it is both appropriate and necessary to rely on a pragmatic justification of belief.

In examining James's argument, we may note that, contrary to the way in which he is usually interpreted, James's view in "The Will to Believe" is not that the option to believe in God is, *simpliciter*, a genuine one. For while it meets the conditions of being forced and momentous, one further condition remains to be fulfilled. For the option to believe in God to be genuine, it must also be live. But liveness is a personal matter, and we must each determine whether the issue of God's existence is a live one for ourselves. While this may seem to be a small consideration, in fact, as we shall see, it has important implications for James's debate with the scientific rationalist.

Indeed, it may seem that those implications are disastrous for James. James's pragmatic justification for believing in God applies only on condition that the religious option is found to be live. But, of course, the scientific rationalist is unlikely to view religion as a live option. Thus, it appears from the way in which James has set up his argument that he has abrogated, from the outset, the challenge of addressing the scientific rationalist, and has therefore opted out of any genuine debate. This conclusion is fortified by the fact that James seems entirely willing to admit that his pragmatic justification of religious belief is quite limited in its appeal. He candidly announces in "The Will to Believe" that his remarks are addressed to the "saving remnant" alone; and he even excuses those who do not find religion in any way attractive from further participation in his argument (WB, 30). Since James does not address his argument only to religious believers, but tenders it to all individuals who are at least open to religious belief, he is not exactly preaching to the choir. Nevertheless, it is unusual, and in this context, particularly problematic, for a philosopher to admit at the outset that his argument, by its very nature, will be persuasive only to an audience which is already relatively sympathetic.

Has James, then, by virtue of the way in which he has set up the conditions of the discussion, essentially turned his back on the scientific rationalist, and thus rendered his argument in "The Will to Believe" largely superfluous? Although it may at first appear so, we shall see, upon fuller examination of the context and the point of his argument, that such a conclusion is not warranted.

First, let us look at James's broader, more rhetorical aims in "The Will to Believe." James's purpose in this essay was not only to develop a more technical philosophical position with regard to the scientific rationalist. He was also, on a more practical level, trying to assist those persons who felt attracted to religion, but whose commitment to being "rational" and "scientific" inhibited their tendency to believe—or as James puts it, "paraly[zed] their native capacity for faith" (WB, 7). James wanted to help these individuals discard unwarranted constraints on what he considered their healthy and appropriate attraction to religion. In this context, then, in terms of the impact James hoped to have on his audience, his choice, in "The Will to Believe," to address only those who already hold religion to be a live option is one which is both effective and judicious. After all, it is from among the people who hold religion as a live option that we may find those who have the most difficulty in dealing with their doubts; and it is those who have doubts who would find James's justification of religious belief to be of most use. Indeed, the people for whom religion is a dead option are not troubled by doubts, since they find in religion nothing to attract them. Presumably, then, they would find James's argument to be of no personal interest.

This point having been made, however, let us remember that James was not just trying to assist people with their personal religious quandaries. He was also trying to deal with the philosophical challenge posed by the scientific rationalist. And in terms of this second goal, given that James directs his argument exclusively to those who hold religious belief as a live option (a group from which scientific rationalists exclude themselves), we must still ask whether James simply has declined to engage with the scientific rationalist, and whether, therefore, the scientific rationalist maintains the philosophical advantage over him. In spite of appearances, I suggest that James has not ignored the scientific rationalist's challenge. Indeed, James's approach to the problem at hand is not unique in his work. On other issues as well, it is not unusual to find claims or strategies on James's part which, in some way or other, appear to be philosophical compromises, but which, after they are more fully understood, turn out to be the vehicles by which he shepherds the discussion at hand to a deeper and more subtle level of discourse.[28]

How does this point apply in the current context? While James does not develop the following argument explicitly, I suggest it is one which captures and more fully develops the meaning of what he is trying to achieve in "The Will to Believe." James is not objecting to the mere fact that the scientific rationalist would reject the pragmatic argument for religious belief. Rather, and quite subtly, James aims to show that the scientific rationalist unjustifiably holds a belief policy which prevents even the *consideration* of the

religious option as a live possibility, and that this in turn renders such an individual incapable of adequately and fully
understanding the pragmatic argument. For without accepting the religious option as live, or put another way, without
having at least a sincere emotional investment in religion
as a viable possibility, scientific rationalists would not be
inclined to explore the deeper dimensions of the meaning of
religious claims; they would not come to understand the
more subtle relations between those claims and the constellation of their established beliefs, commitments, and desires.
Without accepting the religious option as live, it would not
be possible for the scientific rationalist to imagine, with the
measure of vividness and intensity available to those more
religiously inclined, what it means for God to exist; what
it might be like to be supported by Him, to join in communion with Him, and to have the meaning of one's life
genuinely transcend the sum of its mundane particulars.[29]
And if it is impossible for scientific rationalists fully to imagine these things, it is no more possible for them to imagine
what the pragmatic consequences of believing in God might
be. One may, of course, verbalize propositions about these
matters in the context of an abstract discussion. But without the appropriate emotional investment, that is to say,
without accepting religion as a live option, one cannot fully
consider them, or appreciate the role they might play in
one's life.

James's argument against the scientific rationalist, then,
amounts to this: To fully appreciate the pragmatic magnitude of the meaning of God's existence, and thus to understand the pragmatic justification of religious belief, the subject must sincerely hold the religious option as a live one.
But to hold the religious option as a live one is, of course,
precisely what the scientific rationalist is unwilling to do.
James does not fault the scientific rationalists for not accepting the pragmatic argument for believing in God. He faults
them, rather, for refusing to understand that argument.

The following passage illustrates how James applies his point to one of his most outspoken scientific rationalist opponents, W. K. Clifford. While James refers here specifically to Christians, for our purposes we may take him to be referring to any religious individual:

> When the Cliffords tell us how sinful it is to be Christians on such "insufficient evidence," insufficiency is really the last thing they have in mind. For them the evidence is absolutely sufficient, only it makes the other way. They believe so completely in an anti-christian order of the universe that there is no living option: Christianity is a dead hypothesis from the start. (WB, 21–22)

In response to James's argument against the scientific rationalist, it might be held that he has conflated the logical reasons for believing a proposition with the psychological readiness for believing it. It might be argued that from a strictly logical perspective, it is not necessary personally to hold God's existence to be a live option in order fully to understand that belief, and understand what the consequences of holding that belief might be. If the existence of God entails certain consequences, such that belief in Him is a forced and momentous option, anyone ought to be able to see this, whether or not they have the feelings necessary to make the religious option a personally live one for themselves.

From a strictly logical perspective, this is a valid objection to James's position. But the objection misses the fact that James is not approaching philosophical issues from a strictly logical perspective, nor does he think we should. The question of the existence of God, when viewed not as a problem in logic, epistemology, or theology, but as a problem in life, calls for more than a disinterested and purely intellectual response. This is why James holds that unless one has a real interest in the existence of God, unless one has accepted the live possibility of God's existence—emotionally as well as cognitively—one will be unable to understand (in the rich sense of understanding he has in mind) the full magnitude and meaning of the options available for belief. In sum, then, James's goal is to show that the scientific rationalist is guilty not only of subscribing to a flawed epistemic policy, but perhaps even more importantly, the scientific rationalist is guilty of a failure of imagination.

In setting out his views on the nature of philosophy, James contrasts the philosophic way of taking things from other, "dry dogmatic ways" (SPP, 10; see also 11). To ask a person whether they are philosophical, James asserts, is to ask: "Is there space and air in your mind, or must your companions gasp for breath whenever they talk with you?" (EPH, 4). James describes the activity of doing philosophy as involving "the habit of always seeing an alternative, of not taking the usual for granted, of making conventionalities fluid again, of imagining foreign states of mind" (EPH, 4).

Appreciating James's conception of philosophy will enable us better to understand what he finds most objectionable about the position of the scientific rationalist. He thinks that the scientific rationalist is unphilosophical, in the most important sense of the term—for the scientific rationalist has criteria for the justification of belief which are so restrictive that they will not allow the full imaginative consideration of all the possibilities.[30] James puts it elegantly in the following passage. (We may substitute "scientific rationalism" for "intellectualism" here):

> If the [religious] hypothesis *were* true . . . then pure intellectualism, with its veto on our making willing advances, would be an absurdity; and some participation of our sympathetic nature would be logically required. (WB, 31)[31]

To conclude our discussion of "The Will to Believe," then, we have seen that James's aim in this essay is twofold. First, it is to establish the pragmatic justification for religious belief; and second, it is to demonstrate the impoverishment of the position of the scientific rationalist. Against the scientific rationalist, James shows that those who hold this position miss the opportunity to hold religion as a genuine option, because they fail to accept that option as live. Moreover, they miss the momentous consequences which follow from religious belief. And finally, under the guise of rationality, the scientific rationalist subscribes to belief policies which are unimaginative and ultimately irrational.

3

Preconceptual Knowledge

A central element of James's philosophy of religion is his emphasis on experience, as opposed to conceptual thought, as the primary and most significant source of religious knowledge. James presents a formidable challenge to more traditional philosophical approaches to the question of religious knowledge, by defending the possibility of preconceptual modes of apprehending the divine. In this chapter, I shall develop the implications of James's position, and address some of the interesting and provocative epistemological questions which it raises. I shall consider religious experience in general, as well as its more dramatic mystical forms.

James's defense of experience as a direct source of religious knowledge is firmly grounded in his more general epistemology and metaphysics. Throughout his philosophy, and most explicitly developed in *Some Problems of Philosophy* and *Essays in Radical Empiricism*, James argues for the epistemic primacy of experience. James holds that the intellectual, conceptual functions of the mind, whatever their considerable usefulness in helping us meet our practical needs, are derivative from, and of secondary importance to, the flux of experience. Concepts fail to penetrate into reality or provide the level of disclosure of which experience is capable. Rather they distort, and render static, the reality of the flux of experience.

James's more general views on experience are particularly relevant to his appraisal of the limitations of philosophical discourse in the area of religion, most notably its "hollowness and irrelevancy" (VRE, 360). James holds that "[r]eligious language clothes itself in such poor symbols as our life affords" (VRE, 18), but ultimately, religious knowledge must transcend the limitation of concepts. Indeed, in support of the primacy of experiential over conceptual approaches to religion, when he was asked whether any belief in God he personally might hold was based on philosophical argument, James replied, "emphatically no" (LWJ, 2:213).

James sometimes likens religious experience to a kind of sense experience, a "sixth sense" for apprehending divine realities, albeit one which is more diffused, deeper, and more general than the other sense modalities (VRE, 55, 58–59, 66, 321). In a passage with which he originally intended to open the Gifford Lectures, James depicts his sense of the unique depth of religious experience and its independence from conceptual understanding:

> Religion is the very inner citadel of human life, and the pretension to translate adequately into spread-out conceptual terms a kind of experience in which intellect, feeling and will, all our consciousness and our subconsciousness together melt in a kind of chemical fusion, would be particularly abhorrent. . . . [N]o so-called philosophy of religion can possibly begin to be an adequate translation of what goes on in the single private man, as he livingly expresses himself in religious faith and act. (TC, 2:329)[1]

While the force of this description might be due more to its metaphorical qualities than its literal meaning, James's basic intention is powerful and clear: not only is religious experience ultimately out of reach of conceptual thought, it is also not subordinate to it—it is not capable of being impugned by propositional arguments. James wrote the following in a note to himself while preparing the Gifford Lectures:

The struggle seems to be that of a less articulate and more profound part of our nature to hold out, and keep itself standing, against the attempts of a more superficial and explicit or loquacious part, to suppress it. . . . I must shape things and argue to the conclusion that a man's religion is the deepest and wisest thing in his life. I must frankly establish the breach between the life of articulate reason, and the push of the subconscious, the irrational instinctive part, which is more vital. . . . In religion the vital needs, the mystical overbeliefs . . . proceed from an ultra-rational region. They are *gifts.* It is a question of *life,* of living in these gifts or not living. . . . (TC, 2:328)[2]

Many besides James, most notably those in the mystical tradition, have sought to identify a level of knowledge in the sphere of religion which transcends the limitations of conceptual thought. James quotes and cites many of them in *Varieties.* Indeed, James highlights mystical experience as the most compelling form of religious experience. In contrasting mystical experiences to conceptual understanding, in one of his more startling remarks, James claims that "not conceptual speech, but music rather, is the element through which we are best spoken to by mystical truth. Many mystical scriptures are indeed little more than musical compositions" (VRE, 333).[3] In making this claim, James is not suggesting that mystical experience is non-cognitive. Rather, he is invoking a notion of understanding which is more primary than propositional understanding. Our connection with God, as James puts it, is on "that subtle edge of things where speech and thought expire" (WB, 98). When one derives knowledge in this direct experiential manner, James believes, one may not be able to articulate what is known, but one is, nevertheless, immediately acquainted with a deeper level of reality.[4]

More recently, in our own time, Jewish theologian Abraham Joshua Heschel joins James in drawing analogies between music and religious experience. While Heschel is like James in that his remarks are more poetic than precise, this is entirely consonant with the point he is trying to make:

> The only language that seems to be compatible with the wonder and mystery of being is the language of music. Music is more than just expressiveness. It is rather a reaching out toward a realm that lies beyond the reach of verbal propositions. Verbal expression is in danger of being taken literally and of serving as a substitute for insight. Words become slogans, slogans become idols. But music is a refutation of human finality. Music is an antidote to higher idolatry.[5]

I find the position held by James and Heschel to be particularly challenging for what it implies. To posit the superiority—both epistemic and moral—of "the irrational instinctive part" of our minds (James), "beyond the reach of verbal propositions" (Heschel), diminishes our most entrenched conception of ourselves, embedded in our intellectual traditions and social institutions, as beings whose most significant and most honorable dimension is our rationality.[6] In particular, this view challenges many established beliefs about the objectivity of knowledge claims.

One natural response to a view such as this might be to grant that both religious and musical experiences may be beautiful, inspiring, uplifting, and have a host of other beneficial psychological and even moral effects. But many may insist that such subjective and inarticulable experiences cannot be genuinely cognitive. They will hold that for a psychological state to be an instance of knowledge, it must be capable of conceptual articulation, and the claims it involves must be open to conventional, objective standards of evidence. Indeed, a critic might well claim that the defining mark of cognitivity is its objective character, the very heart of which distinguishes it from the subjective and personal qualities of experiences like those in music and religion.

However well-entrenched and even appealing the critic's position may be, it seems to me to overlook significant dimensions of human cognition which philosophers ought more fully to recognize. There is a wide array of knowledge which is not propositional, or at least not primarily propositional, but rather sensory or intuitive in character. Such knowledge goes far beyond simple perceptions, and often involves subtle judgments; but they are judgments which cannot be reduced just to knowing that a given proposition or set of propositions is true.

In *The Principles of Psychology*, James invokes the distinction, which is now well-known, between "knowledge by acquaintance" and "knowledge about."[7] "Knowledge about" is propositional knowledge, while "knowledge by acquaintance" is experiential. To have knowledge about an apple, for example, involves accepting a certain set of propositions about its color, weight, size, flavor, etc. To be acquainted with the apple, on the other hand, is to have directly experienced its look, smell, or taste, etc. James uses the notion of knowledge by acquaintance to develop his argument in *Varieties*. He provides a rather homely, but effective, example of the distinctive depth of personal, experiential knowledge, when he utilizes al-Ghazzali's illustration of the difference between experiencing drunkenness or abstinence, as opposed to having merely propositional knowledge about these states (VRE, 319–20). Developing James's point, we can well imagine that there might be a one-to-one correspondence between the sentences used to describe drunkenness by both a person who has been drunk and one who has not. Individuals without the requisite personal experience might be able to make the same verbal claims as the experienced individual—for they might have been coached, or known a lot of individuals who drink too much; they might have read or memorized accounts of what it is like to be drunk; they may have studied the physiological chemistry of drunken states, etc. But no amount of propositional knowl-

edge, however extensive, can substitute for direct experience. The person who has actually experienced drunkenness
will have a level of knowledge of which the pretender is incapable, for this individual will have personal experience of
the drunken feelings as well as their attendant associations.[8]

As James pointed to the "gaping contrast between the
richness of life and the poverty of all possible formulas"
which are used to describe it (TC, 2:127), we may easily
identify other instances of sensory knowledge for which
conceptual description is inadequate. On the basis of experience, for example, one can recognize the smell of cinnamon
or the taste of claret; one can develop a feel for a language,
or for computers, or the stock market, or for one's chil-
dren or spouse. The gymnast, dancer, or diver develops a
kinesthetic self-awareness, and through experience and attention to that experience, has a sense, not reducible to a
set of propositions, of the appropriate timing and effort
required for various maneuvers. The person of wide experience with music, art, or literature knows, through stored
sensory information and a wealth of associations unavailable
to a less cultivated counterpart, that something sounds like
Mozart, looks like a Kandinsky, or is probably a passage
from Tolstoy. And it is fair to say, I think, that all other
things being equal, the person with the wider experience,
with the greater degree of breadth, multitude, and modula-
tion of experience, with the most extensive array of layers of
association and inter-association, will be wiser and have the
deeper knowledge. Experience, sensitivity, and appreciation
are the relevant factors here, not the assent to a set of propositional truths and the ability logically to manipulate them.[9]

It is worth noting that the notion of preconceptual, experiential knowledge functions just as powerfully in descriptions of certain stages of scientific thought as it does
in daily life. To some this fact may be unsettling, if they
share the common belief that science and religion are fun-

damentally opposed in their intellectual methods and commitments. Nevertheless, examples of experiential, preconceptual knowledge from the history of science are quite common. To mention a few, Einstein, for instance, describes the first stages of his own creative scientific thought as pre-logical and pre-linguistic. He asserts that his thinking at these stages relies on "visual" and "muscular" elements.[10] To take another example, a frequently cited anecdote in the history of science is the account, in the field of organic chemistry, of Friedrich Kekulé's path-breaking discovery of (what is now called) the benzine ring. The ring-like structure of this chemical became clear in a dream in which Kekulé envisioned a snake seizing hold of its own tail.[11] But if, as seems obvious, Kekulé learned something (that is to say, gained knowledge) in his dream, then this incident constitutes additional evidence that genuine knowledge may be intuitive and non-propositional.[12]

It is, of course, possible to respond to reports such as Kekulé's and Einstein's by claiming that the experiences they describe are merely pre-cognitive. It might be argued that these experiences constitute a necessary step in a process which eventuates in knowledge, but that they are not noetic in themselves. But it seems to me that it begs the question to insist, with no additional justification, that experiences like those described by Kekulé, Einstein, and others we have mentioned should not be considered noetic. Short of considerably developed argumentation to support the point, it is only by assuming that knowledge must contain propositional or conceptual elements that one would be inclined to reject intuitive knowledge of the sort in question. But why *must* propositional knowledge be the only kind of knowledge? Given the data, I suggest that the burden of proof lies not on those who accept non-propositional knowledge, but on those who reject it. The reasonable course is not to reject reports like Einstein's and the others out of hand as conceptually confused, simply because they challenge more entrenched philosophical positions. Rather, it is to see if we can broaden the range of received philosophical conceptions of knowledge to account for what seems credible, or at least suggestive and intriguing, in the reports before us.

Nor is it convincing simply to claim that the examples from Einstein and Kekulé show only that the "context of discovery" is different from the "context of justification," and that since Einstein's and Kekulé's experiences do not provide logical justifications for their claims, they cannot be said to constitute knowledge.[13] For the distinction between the context of justification and the context of discovery has itself been seriously challenged as being an unrealistic bifurcation which some philosophers have imposed, from without, on the complex processes in which working scientists engage.[14]

Further support for the notion of preconceptual understanding has recently come from Mark Johnson, in *The Body in the Mind*.[15] In this book Johnson argues against the dominant tradition of "objectivist," truth-conditional semantics and in favor of what he calls a "semantics of understanding." On the basis of his examination of both empirical and philosophical work in semantics, Johnson aims to show that structures of imagination and understanding, generated from bodily experience, function as both guides to our reasoning, and constituent elements in the meaning of a wide range of concepts about the world. The key to his position lies in the concept of an "image schema," which he defines as "a recurring dynamic pattern of our perceptual interactions and motor programs that gives coherence and structure to our experience."[16] Examining somatic experiences of balance, force, containment, movement, and others, Johnson makes a convincing case for non-propositional, experiential, and figurative dimensions of meaning. This is what he says about force:

We begin to grasp the meaning of physical force from the day we are born (or even before). We have bodies that are acted upon by "external" and "internal" forces such as gravity, light, heat, wind, bodily processes, and the obtrusion of other physical objects. Such interactions constitute our first encounters with forces, and they reveal patterned recurring relations between ourselves and our environment. Such patterns develop as meaning structures through which our world begins to exhibit a measure of coherence, regularity, and intelligibility.

Soon . . . we develop patterns for interacting forcefully with our environment. . . . These patterns are embodied and give coherent, meaningful structure to our physical experience at a *preconceptual* level, though we are eventually taught names for at least some of these patterns, and can discuss them in the abstract. Of course, we formulate a *concept* of "force," which we can explicate in propositional terms. But its meaning—the meaning it identifies—goes deeper than our conceptual and propositional understanding.[17]

The significance of Johnson's position lies not so much in his claim that cognition includes somatic elements, though that is certainly of great interest. The point of importance for our purposes is the more radical one—namely, that those somatic structures may be understood as themselves non-propositional embodiments of knowledge. If Johnson has established that the meaning of some concepts lies deeper than our conceptual and propositional understanding, then the recent semantic and empirical studies in the cognitive sciences which he brings to bear in support of his own position may be used to support James's view as well.

It is interesting to note in passing that Johnson credits some recent Continental philosophers, notably Heidegger and Gadamer, for having provided antecedents for his

more general conclusions in favor of the interpretive nature of objectivity and knowledge.[18] He also acknowledges
a romantic tradition in semantics, characterized by an anti-
reductionist view of meaning, and represented by such
thinkers as Samuel Taylor Coleridge, I. A. Richards, and
Max Black.[19] Johnson correctly points out that Anglo-
American analytic philosophy typically has shown little interest in personalized aspects of meaning.[20] He ought not
to have counted out the Americans so quickly, however.
For had he looked further back into the American tradition, he would have seen the very central importance of the
pragmatists in the history of positions such as his own. For
instance, a fundamental tenet of James's philosophy is that
concepts derive their meaning from our purposes and interests. In addition, James's theory of truth, his conception of rationality, and the pragmatic dimension of his
analysis of reality, are views of which Johnson's position are
particularly reminiscent.[21] I have brought Johnson into this
discussion, however, not because he follows James, but because of the new evidence (especially empirical evidence) he
brings to bear which supports James's position.

Let us look again at music, for we have still more to learn
from it. Along with James's and Heschel's views, we may
add the more recent view of Catholic theologian Richard
Viladesau. Viladesau describes himself as continuing the
mainstream of the Christian tradition, including Martin
Luther and Thomas Aquinas, among others, in expounding
the view that in some of its forms, music "convey[s] a sense
of spiritual reality."[22] He holds that the experience of beauty
is "revelatory of the transcendent."[23] That revelation is
possible, Viladesau maintains, because music is "in itself
a mirror of God's beauty, and thus a means of reaching
the soul directly with a message about God which is inexpressible in words."[24] "[M]usic raises the mind to God
because it reflects and expresses the beautiful order of creation itself."[25]

Holding the opposite position, we find more positivistically-minded philosophers, like John Hospers. In *Meaning and Truth in the Arts,* Hospers contends that while music may evoke profound responses, it is not a source of knowledge.[26] It is interesting that Hospers builds his claim upon the same distinction which James has utilized for the opposite purpose, namely, the distinction between "knowledge about," or propositional knowledge, and "knowledge by acquaintance."[27] Hospers maintains that so-called "knowledge by acquaintance" is not really knowledge at all. For to have knowledge of something, he maintains, involves more than just being aware of its qualities. It is only when that awareness (the flavor of an apple, for example) enables you to assert some propositions about the object (that the apple is sweet, for example) that you then have genuine knowledge. Applying his view to music, he claims:

> When we hear music, we have deeper, richer acquaintance, not knowledge—it is not the function of music to give us that. . . . [Propositional knowledge] is the task of the special sciences.[28]

But why accept Hospers's position? He excludes acquaintance with (awareness of) an object's qualities as a form of knowledge because to be so acquainted does not involve any propositional claims. But he simply assumes that knowledge necessarily does involve making propositional claims. Since Hospers defines knowledge as necessarily being propositional from the outset, for him to reject acquaintance as a form of knowledge is simply to beg the question. The issue is hardly whether propositional knowledge must be propositional—the denial of that would be self-contradictory—but rather whether there is reason to believe that another sort of knowledge, which is not propositional in nature, is possible.

D. W. Gotshalk, in *Art and the Social Order,*[29] offers a far more sensitive and nuanced analysis. He contends that literary fiction, for example, may give us insights into life, by illuminating such phenomena as our choices, limitations, and temptations, to name a few. Fictional portrayals may give us *a feel for* general truths about life, which has a level of depth and impact which no merely propositional articulation could achieve. He argues that paintings also present truths non-propositionally. They may "give us an idealized and simplified version of natural aspects on the perceptual level, just as the mathematical laws of theoretical mechanics incidentally give us an idealized and simplified version of natural aspects on a conceptual level." And "[m]usic can give us amazing insights into the qualities of innumerable nameless emotions, as well as into the qualities of innumerable nameable ones: rage, eagerness, love, tenderness, fervor, and the like."[30]

I am not sure why Gotshalk goes only so far as to say that music may illuminate only our emotional states. If paintings can give us insights into objective reality, might not music engender such insights as well? Might it not be the case that music can reflect, illustrate, or illuminate features which *seem*, at least, to have objective pertinency? Schopenhauer thought it could. "The composer reveals the inner nature of the world" he claims, "and expresses the deepest wisdom in a language which his reason does not understand."[31] Beethoven also thought so, and other composers have thought so as well. Beethoven spoke of music as revelatory; and by this he meant not just that we achieve greater insights into our inner life, but that through music we are somehow able to get in contact with a level of reality more profound than words can express.[32] Of course Beethoven is not a philosopher, and so one may be tempted to dismiss his views as philosophically naive. But does it make sense to reject Beethoven's position just because it challenges entrenched philosophical views? Might it not be more appropriate to re-examine our philosophy? Since Beethoven represents, arguably, the pinnacle of human musical genius, should not philosophers at least be open to the idea that Beethoven is in a privileged position to say what music can and cannot achieve? The alternative is to say that Beethoven did not really understand the nature of what he was doing.

To summarize our discussion thus far, the key issue has been whether the experiences we have been considering—whether they be musical or religious—can be said actually to give knowledge. It would certainly not be appropriate to treat religious experiences as untrustworthy simply because they are religious. In non-religious and every-day contexts, given the appropriate conditions, we feel fully justified in trusting our experience in claiming to know common empirical facts. Why should we treat religious experience differently? If, against the perennial laments of the sceptic, many find it eminently reasonable to believe in the objective existence of physical objects, might it not be reasonable to override at least the automatic, wholesale varieties of religious scepticism as well? This is not to suggest that any degree of scepticism is out of place. For in the case of religion, as in any other domain in which knowledge claims are made, it is necessary to have criteria for distinguishing between veridical and non-veridical experiences. Nevertheless, we ought to acknowledge that just as it is wise as a general rule to honor our robust faith in the existence of the external world, it may be equally appropriate to honor our sense of a deeper spiritual reality. I suggest that it is appropriate to take seriously whatever indications we may have concerning religious truths. That such indications may be meager may attest only to the limits of our cognitive abilities in the context of the immensity of the questions before us. Moreover, as James also suggests, who is to say that our need for something to be true may not be a good indication that it is so? While this is a complex and difficult claim to defend, still such a possibility seems especially poignant in light of the extraordinary power of many individuals' religious yearnings and sensibilities. In chapter 4, we shall examine more fully whether an individual's emotional responses may be regarded as in any way constituting evidence for religious truths. Let me just say now that it is a foolish and superficial parody of the ideal of rationality to insist that in our struggle with religious questions, we should wait for conventional propositional knowledge and conventional methods of proof; methods which to this point have given no indication of providing, or of even being able to provide, adequate answers.

A few moments' introspection will reveal a broad and deep range of human responsiveness which lies beyond the linear, logical, conceptual domain. Indeed, the emotional, physical, temperamental, aesthetic, and spiritual dimensions of life comprise the greatest part of our existence. Family attachments, physical bonding, feelings of loss and mourning, identifications with our traditions and history, spiritual yearnings, the felt nourishment of solitude, the sense of the body's daily rhythms and the wider cadences of the life cycle, our deep feeling for natural beauty—these and other such phenomena indicate a profundity and strength of human responsiveness which extend far beyond the domain of scientific, rational, or literal discourse. Given this fact, it seems gratuitous to take our deepest sensitivities, preferences, and desires and consider them as pre-eminently subject to validation by intellectual criteria alone. The specific application of this point to the question of religion is as follows: just as it would not make sense to hold that the fulfillment of our aesthetic, emotional, social, or biological sensitivities must be legitimated by the intellect, it does not make sense to hold that the fulfillment of our religious sensitivities must depend on their intellectual acceptability, even if our religious sensitivities, perhaps more obviously than the others, lead us to make metaphysical claims. What possible justification could there be for privileging the intellect in this way? It is far more judicious to acknowledge intellectual sensitivities as one of numerous human capacities, without considering them hegemonic.

Of course, even if we make the choice to reject wholesale religious scepticism, we are still left with the challenge of finding answers to our religious questions. My point has been just that the respect for religious sensibility leaves us open to the possibility that religious experience has some sort of objective pertinency, even if we cannot yet fully specify the mechanism to explain it, or precisely what the tests of its adequacy might be.

How might the veridicality of religious experience be assessed? It would seem that if experiential religious knowledge is preconceptual, it is ineluctably mute, and as such it is beyond the pale of intellectual manipulation or assessment.[33] As James puts it, "the attempt to demonstrate by purely intellectual processes the truth of the deliverances of direct religious experience is absolutely hopeless" (VRE, 359; see also WB, 105); religious experiences "are indestructible by intellectual arguments and criticisms" (VRE, 543; see also 302, 551). But if we take these claims at face value, we are forced to ask whether religious experiential knowledge, as James understands it, in any way resembles more ordinary forms of knowledge with which we are familiar. In short, the most salient question which arises from James's position is this: what sort of knowledge is it in which conceptual thought has no foothold in the relationship between what is experienced, and what is alleged to be known?

Religious revelation may be regarded as the clearest and most interesting form of experiential knowledge of God. In cases of revelation, it is held, God is felt, directly experienced—religious truths are present-to-hand.[34] James offers a continuum of experiences which he thinks may be counted, in varying degrees, as revelatory. Mystical states represent the highest end-point on the continuum of such revelatory experiences.[35] James identifies two characteristics as being definitive of a mystical experience: its ineffability and its noetic quality (VRE, 302).[36] Insofar as they are ineffable, James believes, mystical experiences are "more like states of feeling than like states of intellect" (VRE, 302). And to say that mystical experiences have a noetic quality is to say that they appear to the mystic as having cognitive value: they are regarded as "states of insight into depths of truth unplumbed by the discursive intellect" (VRE, 302). One excellent example of the coalescence of both the affective and cognitive aspects of the mystical experience can be found in the following exquisite description by Thomas Merton:

> It was as if I had been suddenly illuminated by being blinded by the manifestation of God's presence. The reason why this light was blinding and neutralizing was that there was and could be simply nothing in it of sense or imagination. . . . [T]his awareness . . . disarmed all images, all metaphors, and cut through the whole skein of species and phantasms with which we naturally do our thinking. It ignored all sense experience in order to strike directly at the heart of truth, as if a sudden and immediate contact had been established between my intellect and the Truth Who was now physically really and substantially before me on the altar. But this contact was not something speculative and abstract: it was concrete and experimental and belonged to the order of knowledge, yes, but more still to the order of love. . . . It was love as clean and direct as vision: and flew straight to the possession of the Truth it loved.[37]

Philosophers of a scientific rationalist persuasion are profoundly sceptical about any such supposedly non-conceptual revelatory experience. George Nakhnikian, for instance, in a symposium on religious experience and truth, offers an assessment of the idea of revelation which is typical of the resistance, if not animosity, with which these philosophers approach the concept of the ineffable knowledge of God. Nakhnikian argues that the concept of knowledge by revelation is essentially a meaningless one, because it involves the incoherent notion that the subject's experiences of the divine are inexpressible in conceptual terms. With regard to mysticism in particular, Nakhnikian argues that the mystics' claims must be rejected, because their putative revelations are incapable of being conceptualized and described:

> [T]he mystic's claims can have no epistemological validity. For the incommunicable residue [of the mystic's experience], which is the heart of the matter from the mystic's point of view, cannot be discussed at all. "What we can't say, we can't say, and we can't whistle it either." We cannot philosophize about what we cannot say. This, in the final analysis, is the only philosophical statement we can make about it.[38]

Nakhnikian, like other philosophers who repudiate mystical experience because of its ineffability, bases his negative judgment on an overly narrow and incorrect assumption about what may count as philosophically relevant in assessing the mystic's claims. The core of Nakhnikian's argument is his claim that "we cannot philosophize about what we cannot say." But is this true? What can be meant by the notion of what we cannot say? It is true that mystics report that their experiences cannot be described directly—language is incapable of capturing what they are like. But this in no way entails that there is nothing left to think or say about them. For the mystics regard their experiences as incomparable, supreme, and consummatory occasions in their lives, ones which can be sustained in only certain sorts of discourse and which cohere with only certain sets of other beliefs. While James makes it a point to acknowledge that not all mystical or other claims based on religious experience are veridical, he also provides some circumstantial criteria which he thinks provides evidence in their favor. Speaking of the wider category of religious experience, in which mystical experience is included, James makes the following claim:

> I find it preposterous to suppose that if there be a feeling of unseen reality shared by large numbers of best men in their best moments, responded to by other men in their "deep" moments, good to live by, strength-giving,—I find it preposterous, I say, to suppose that the goodness of that feeling for living purposes should be held to carry no objective significance. . . .[39]

James's suggestion is supported, more recently, by Daya Krishna, who makes the following claim:

> The capacity for inner freedom, abiding joy, and relevant response to external situations is so pre-eminent and abundant in spiritual persons that compared to them, ordinary, normal persons appear as deficient human beings.[40]

Among spiritual persons, the lives of the mystics are particularly exemplary in terms of the categories to which James and Krishna refer. While one might be tempted to understand Krishna's claim to be pointing to a "deficiency" of "normal" persons only in the moral domain, in fact Krishna would agree with James that the mystic appears to be in an epistemically privileged position as well. While the points made by James and Krishna are not, and are not intended to be, conclusive, their considerations are suggestive and important. Although the veridicality of mystical experience is not susceptible to direct test (at least not by the non-mystic), there is much in the way of indirect evidence, concerning the mystic's overall belief system, actions, and quality of life, which is relevant to its assessment.

While indirect evidence might not be sufficient to prove, conclusively, that the mystics' experiences are veridical, why might it not help establish the probability of the truth of their claims? Why must the epistemic situation in regard to the mystic be as impossible as Nakhnikian depicts it to be, especially given the unique nature of the mystic's claims? Surely there is considerable precedent in ordinary, non-religious contexts for appealing to indirect evidence to assess beliefs. For example, if Jones alleges that Smith robbed him, and Smith denies it, and there are no other witnesses involved, often we can still make a reasonable judgment about what really happened. We base our judgment on those facts about which we do have direct knowledge, and which provide circumstantial evidence for resolving the question at hand. Such facts include, for example, the credibility of Jones and Smith, the internal consistency of each of their reports, the consistency of their reports with any other relevant facts, the motives they might have to act the way they do, the reasons they might have to prevaricate, and so on.

All this said, there is one final, and even more powerful dimension of religious experience, as James understands it, which I should like to explore. James believes that mystical revelation is the purest and most perfect direct knowledge of the divine, but he is also reaching toward an idea which is more difficult and more profound. The end-point to which I believe James aspires, the apotheosis of his philosophy of religion, lies in a concept of revelation which goes deeper than mere knowledge of the divine, however direct, and involves the notion of the subject identifying with and participating in God's existence itself.

I shall discuss James's religious metaphysics more fully in chapter 7. At this point, let us simply note that James holds that God is a "wider self," or universal "mother sea" of experience, in which each individual participates (VRE, 399–408, 543). To have the highest form of religious experience, on James's view, is to become aware of one's participation in that "wider self" of universal consciousness with which one is continuous (VRE, 405). Thus the achievement in religious experience is at once to actualize one's knowledge of, as well as one's conscious unification with, the divine. James states:

> Remember that the whole point [of religion] lies in really *believing* that through a certain point or part in you you coalesce and are identical with the Eternal. This seems to be the *saving* belief both in Christianity and in Vedantism. . . . The more original religious life is always lyric . . . and its essence is to dip into another kingdom, to feel an invisible order. . . .[41]

On James's view, then, in religious revelation, the subject not only comes to know God, but also acknowledges and thereby perfects a metaphysical unification with Him. The distinction between merely knowing God (through revelation, in the narrow sense), and participating in God's existence (through revelation in the broad sense, as James conceives it), is momentous. For however great an epistemological achievement it might be to know God, the actual conscious participation in God's divinity would be a metaphysical achievement conferring such profound moral and spiritual authority that mere knowledge of God (however impressive that is in itself) pales by comparison.

It might be objected that given James's religious ontology, it is not the fact that one has a religious experience which effects unification with the divine. For if, as James contends, we are by nature part of a wider, more pervasive sea of experience, then we participate in the divine by virtue of that fact alone. The reality of our divine participation does not depend upon our actually being cognizant of, or even desiring such an affiliation.

The validity of this objection hinges on what is meant by "participation" in the divine. Granting the fundamental fact of James's religious ontology—that one participates in the divine whether or not one is aware of it—it remains the case that differing levels of participation are possible. Notice that in the case of some relations in which an individual participates, the knowledge that one is in the relation engenders in one an additional, self-regarding property, which in its turn amplifies and enriches the level of participation itself. To use an example outside religion to illustrate this point, compare on the one hand, a sister and brother who know that they are siblings, and on the other hand, a sister and brother who are not aware of their relationship to one another. The sister's feelings about and behavior toward her brother, all other things being equal, will be quite different, depending on whether she is aware of her brother's biological relationship to her. If she is aware of her true relationship to her brother, she will, all other things being equal, feel and act in ways (whether positively or negatively) which more fully embody that relationship. Similarly in a religious context, knowledge of one's ontological status may itself confer upon a person an enriched relationship to the divine. When one recognizes one's own participation in the divine, participation as a bare ontological fact—which by itself may be pragmatically inert—becomes transformed into a living commerce with the divine. Thus, even in the context of James's religious ontology, religious experience can still bring about ontological change in the individual.

Whether or not we accept James's religious metaphysics, I think the suggestions in his religious epistemology can be developed and assessed on their own. The aim of this chapter has been to demonstrate the strength of James's view that religious experience is a source of knowledge of the divine. James has helped us more fully to understand how preconceptual knowledge is possible, and shown us what its significance might be. This is a substantial step beyond the restrictive view of the scientific rationalist, and the conceptual abstractions of the speculative philosopher as well.

───── 4 ─────

The Cognitive Value Of Feelings

James describes himself in *Varieties* as "bent on rehabili-
tating the element of feeling in religion" (VRE, 395). He
believes, quite correctly, that religious emotions are characteristically deeply felt. The experience of awe in the face of
the grandeur of the universe, for example, or the emotions
that accompany the acknowledgement of one's own finitude in a scheme of infinite proportions; the feelings of joy
in appreciation of what is felt to be a divine presence, or of
trust in the face of tragedy or loss, typically hold an abiding
and important place in a person's psychic life.[1] Moreover,
religious feelings are apt to alter profoundly the kind of life
the individual leads. On the basis of such feelings, the subject may make new aesthetic or ethical judgments, as well as
new kinds of practical commitments. But James is not interested in providing only a set of psychological observations
about what religious feelings may be like as subjective states,
or what their practical, moral, or aesthetic benefits may be.
For he believes that states of mind such as "religious rap-
ture," "ontological wonder," or "cosmic emotion" (VRE,
225) may also be deeply significant cognitively—they may
be a means by which the subject recognizes genuine religious truths. That feelings "may be as prophetic and an-
ticipatory of truth as anything else we have," James claims,
"cannot possibly be denied" (ERE, 143).[2] He also believes
that in addition to religious feelings, religious needs may
have cognitive value as well. "[I]f needs of ours outrun the

61

visible universe," James claims, "why *may* not that be a sign that an invisible universe is there?" (WB, 51).

The claim that feelings have cognitive value is a startling and unusual one. It has earned James the admiration of "romantics" and the opprobrium of more literal and scientific rationalist thinkers. For how can a subjective emotion be the basis for objective knowledge? In this chapter we shall examine what James's assertions might mean, and how they might be defended. While it may appear peculiar, if not outrageous, for James to claim that emotions, and even desires or needs, can provide evidence for claims about the existence of a divine reality, we shall see that when properly understood, his suggestions are far more plausible than might be supposed.

Later in this chapter, we shall examine the particular arguments James develops to support his view that feelings have cognitive value. His arguments may best be appreciated, however, by first understanding more fully the scientific rationalist perspective from which his view most severely might be challenged. Let us consider a point by George Nakhnikian, who questions whether feelings can have cognitive significance.[3] Nakhnikian argues that feelings such as "cosmic awe" or "cosmic thankfulness" provide no evidence whatever for the reality of a divine being who has the attributes which would evoke or merit such feelings on our part:

> [I]t is conceivable that our feelings of cosmic thankfulness and cosmic awe have a fitting recipient, but the mere fact of our having the feelings does not support the probability of the hypothesis.[4]

Nakhnikian accepts that we have religious feelings, of course, but he thinks that psychological (for example, Freudian) explanations of them are more plausible than those explanations which require a divine force or being as their source and referent. Nakhnikian is even willing to grant that some religious feelings are, in his words, "vectorial"— that they seem to point outside themselves. But he suggests that this fact does not require that we posit an objective being whose existence would render these feelings appropriate. Nakhnikian interprets the fact that feelings such as awe are "vectorial" to mean only that they "create in those who are experiencing them a need to find symbols adequate for externalizing them."[5] And we may "externalize" them, Nakhnikian holds, simply by acting on the basis of them. Taking an example from his own life, Nakhnikian reports feeling a kind of "cosmic awe" when his infant daughter narrowly escaped a fatal car accident. Rather than positing a supernatural being or property as an appropriate object for his awe, however, Nakhnikian reports that he was satisfied to "externalize his feelings" through his behavior: by expressing particularly tender feelings of love toward his daughter. Thus, he argues, our "vectorial" inner states can find adequate expression without our having to posit divine realities.[6]

Whatever else may be the difficulties with this position, one problem is that Nakhnikian falls prey to the ambiguity of the notion of "externalizing one's feelings." Contrary to Nakhnikian, I suggest that the particular "vectorial" nature of religious awe and other such emotions lies in the subject's strong feeling of relating to a phenomenon or being which is (at least in some ways) separable from and far greater than oneself. The fact that one can "externalize" one's feelings, in Nakhnikian's contracted and trivial sense, by expressing them "objectively" through one's behavior, is irrelevant to the sense of objective reference which is intrinsic to the religious feelings themselves. Of course this is not yet to say that the subject's *sense* of objective reference

is necessarily veridical. It is only to say, at this point, that
the feeling of external reference should not simply be defined away as something else.

I am less concerned with Nakhnikian's position in particular than I am with a type of reasoning, which Nakhnikian exemplifies, by which religious beliefs and emotions are
often too easily dismissed. As we have seen earlier and shall
see more fully below, James reserved some of his strong-
est censure for those views in his own day which share what
I take to be Nakhnikian's basic assumptions. What would
motivate a philosopher to ignore the sense of objective
pertinency which religious feelings typically include? Why
would a philosopher hold that religious feelings *must* be
other than they seem? I believe that the major assumption
behind the tendency to trivialize religious feelings is the
belief that the phenomena or entities to which these feelings are alleged to refer are clearly unreal. But what, in turn,
is the basis for this belief?

While one can go only so far in speculating about any philosopher's motivating assumptions, I suggest that analyses
such as Nakhnikian's and other scientific rationalists' (in
James's day as well as our own) may ultimately rest upon the
way in which they use the principle of parsimony, or as it is
often called, "Ockham's razor." The principle of parsimony
prescribes that when two explanations of the same phenomenon within the same intellectual domain are equally
acceptable in all other respects, it is rational to choose the
more parsimonious one. In terms more directly related to
our discussion of the cognitive value of feelings, the principle of parsimony prescribes that in formulating causal or
other explanations, one ought not to multiply entities unnecessarily.

The opponent of religion applies the principle of parsimony to the analysis of religious feelings in a way which
is clear: if one desires to explain religious feelings as parsi-

moniously as possible, one may do so, and ought to do so, without positing a divine reality. God, as part of an explanatory hypothesis, is simply otiose. We have the feelings—that is certain—but their supposed objective referent is an unwarranted addition. Thus, the scientific rationalist replaces religious explanations of religious feelings with, say, psychological or sociological ones, which appear more philosophically and scientifically respectable.

The principle of parsimony, of course, has been widely utilized in scientific and philosophical reasoning. Indeed, it has been extant in some form or other at least since William of Ockham formulated a version of it in the fourteenth century, and such long durability attests to the fact that it has served well, if in a general way, as a philosophic and scientific principle. But the question we shall ask, and which James asks as well, is whether the principle of parsimony can sustain the weight of the anti-religious claims which it is used to support.

While parsimonious explanations have the advantage of simplicity, it is important to acknowledge that the simplest explanation of a phenomenon is not necessarily the correct one, and hence an over-reliance on a criterion of simplicity is apt to impede intellectual progress. Johannes Kepler comes to mind here: He struggled long and hard to explain his data by positing a simple and obvious circular planetary orbit for Mars. But he finally had to renounce this hypothesis, in order to be open to his discovery that planetary orbits are ellipses—a conclusion not as simple as the hypothesis that they are circles, but one which is nonetheless correct.[7]

It should also be noted that although the criterion of simplicity may be used in a relatively straightforward way in the context of some theories, its meaning is not unambiguous. Indeed, as Carl Hempel has argued, given the complexity of explanatory contexts, no general characterization of simplicity has yet been devised.[8] It follows from this, then, that while the principle of parsimony may function as a good rule of thumb, it is not clear enough or powerful enough to be used by itself to discredit religious (or other) claims.

Granting, however, that the principle of parsimony is often useful, the question still arises as to its relationship to other principles of explanatory adequacy. To appeal to parsimony, all other things being equal, is not to suggest that it is the sole, or even the most important criterion for assessing theories, religious or otherwise. For all things are not always equal, and there are multiple criteria of explanatory adequacy. Gilbert Harman, for example, in his now classic article, "Inference to the Best Explanation," includes the criteria of plausibility and explanatory power, and the degree to which an explanation avoids being ad hoc.[9] Among the many discussions of this topic, Peter Lipton has recently added that we prefer "explanations that specify a mechanism, that are precise, and that contribute to the unification of our overall explanatory scheme."[10] One of Lipton's central aims, moreover, is to distinguish between the likeliest explanation (i.e., the one which is best supported by evidence), and the explanation, which, if it were true, would provide the most understanding.[11] He thus adds an additional, and very interesting, condition of explanatory adequacy: the criterion of providing the most understanding.

Whether or not one wholly agrees with the particular criteria which have been proposed, it is clear that there are a substantial number of criteria of explanatory adequacy. But in the context of multiple criteria, the importance of the principle of parsimony should not be overemphasized. It is only one criterion among many, and even if the principle were itself unproblematic, there would be no reason to think it is primary. Given the uniqueness and complexity of explanatory contexts, the relative importance of parsimony must be determined in each particular case.

Indeed, the choice of the most acceptable explanation is complicated even further by the fact that no hard and fast line can be drawn between the *epistemic* warrant for an explanation and the *pragmatic* justification for believing it. In choosing those members of a set of putative explanations which have even *prima facie* plausibility, we depend on a large set of background beliefs. But such background beliefs are themselves conditioned by our purposes and interests.[12] What counts as an acceptable explanation, then, depends not only on the nature of the phenomenon to be explained, but also on the context in which the explanation is desired—including the degree of knowledge and precision possible in the situation, as well as the needs and purposes of the inquirers.[13]

I suggest that the mistake of the many philosophers who, along with Nakhnikian, approach religion from a scientific rationalist perspective, is to think that the point of religion is to provide a list of existing entities, an inventory of the world's contents, no different in kind, for example, from everyday empirical enumerations of the contents of a room. The difference between religious and secular accounts of the universe, on this view, is that religious accounts (at least theistic ones) include at least one additional entity (God), and additional actions or judgments (God's) which secular accounts leave out, and which are regarded as unnecessary.

In the desire to opt for parsimony, all other things being equal, philosophers who reject religion are often precipitous in judging that all other things *are* equal. They are overly zealous and insensitive in their application of Ockham's razor, and they bring little imagination to bear to try to understand what other criteria of adequacy (explanatory or otherwise) the appeal to divine realities might fulfill. In such an unnecessarily restricted intellectual context, it is no wonder that divine entities or events are rejected as otiose.

Religious hypotheses, if true, offer a unique type and depth of understanding; they uniquely satisfy needs which are different from those satisfied by secular hypotheses. When we ask religious questions we are not searching for a purely intellectual commentary, nor are we asking for the leanest and most austere possible inventory of the contents of the world. We are asking for the profoundest possible explanation, to help us understand and appreciate, as deeply as we can, why we are here; what, if anything, life and existence mean; and how we should behave with regard to them. But the hypotheses which might help answer these normative and teleological questions are precluded if the principle of parsimony is regarded as unproblematic, and as overriding all other criteria of adequacy of theory choice.

While I have questioned the principle of parsimony on epistemological and methodological grounds, James goes even deeper in his level of dissatisfaction with it. It is interesting that he does not reject the principle entirely. Indeed, there are occasions where he appeals to it himself.[14] Nevertheless, James regards as seriously impoverished the ideals of thinking, and underlying that, the conception of the person, which he thinks the principle of parsimony presupposes. In "Remarks on Spencer's Definition of Mind as Correspondence," he expresses his view as follows:

> [T]o the average sense of mankind, whose ideal of mental nature is best expressed by the word "richness," your statistical and cognitive intelligence will seem insufferably narrow, dry, tedious and unacceptable. (EPH, 17)

James often expresses his strong feelings against points of view which are "narrow," "dry," and "tedious." In "Reflex Action and Theism," he claims that the over-utilization of Ockham's razor "blights the development of the intellect" (WB, 104). He amplifies this idea in his criticism of those on whom he splendidly bestows the title "knights of the razor":

The knights of the razor will never form among us more than a sect; but when I see their fraternity increasing in numbers, and, what is worse, when I see their negations acquiring almost as much prestige and authority as their affirmations legitimately claim over the minds of the docile public, I feel as if the influences working in the direction of our mental barbarization were beginning to be rather strong, and needed some positive counteraction. (WB, 105)

When James calls the opponents of religion "knights of the razor," he is expressing his view that their religious scepticism calls for an impoverishment of human experience, while he supports its enrichment. In a letter of 1904, James writes to L. T. Hobhouse that "your bogey is superstition; my bogey is desiccation." Continuing with a passionate, if overstated, defense of the position he took in "The Will to Believe," James claims:

In ["The Will to Believe"] the evil shape was a vision of "Science" in the form of abstraction, priggishness and sawdust, lording it over all. Take the sterilest scientific prig and cad you know, compare him with the richest religious intellect you know, and you would not, any more than I would, give the former the exclusive right of way. (LWJ, 2:208–9)[15]

Perhaps the best way to sum up James's attitude about the principle of parsimony is to reemphasize the fact that thinking is situated in the wider context of the subject's life as a whole, and takes its meaning and purpose from that wider context. To overemphasize parsimony, James believes, is to idealize a desiccated and insipid model of human thinking. In contrast, James offers a more subtle and vigorous conception of thought which includes emotive and imaginative elements. James's insight is that our most important questions cannot even be approached if we presuppose a simplistic model of a linear intelligence which excludes emotional, practical, and spiritual dimensions of the individual.

With this general principle having been laid down, we may now ask, what exactly is James's view of the cognitive status of feelings? Gerald E. Myers suggests that James holds a belief in pre-established harmony between our feelings and the objective world; that for James, "our subjective natures, feelings, emotions and propensities exist as they do because something in reality harmonizes with them. . . ."[16] But Myers considers this position to be "outrageous."[17] Understood in such unqualified and such teleological terms, I can see why Myers would find difficulties with James's position. I should like to suggest, however, that James's view is more subtle than Myers allows. James offers two kinds of argument, neither of which involves a belief in pre-established harmony.[18]

In his first argument, James draws parallels between the most basic feelings and desires which animate both science and religion. He supports religion by suggesting that while its basis is emotional, so also is the basis of science. He argues, moreover, that since scientific judgments built upon that emotional basis have shown themselves to be reliable (in that they have been confirmed), one should not deny the possibility that religious feelings (like wonder or awe) will support judgments equally as successful as scientific ones.

In this sense, religious feelings are best seen as just the starting points upon which our religious beliefs may be developed, and not their ultimate verification. Notice, in his essay "Is Life Worth Living?", the degree to which James qualifies his position; how far he abjures any simple trust in pre-established harmony:

> The inner need of believing that this world of nature is a sign of something more spiritual and eternal than itself is

just as strong and authoritative in those who feel it, as the inner need of uniform laws of causation ever can be in a professional scientific head. The toil of many generations has proved the latter need prophetic. Why *may* not the former one be prophetic too? (WB, 51)

Whatever the advantages of this argument, I think James's more interesting argument is a second, pragmatic one. In this second argument, James makes the case that all other things being equal, religious emotions such as awe and cosmic wonder deserve to be trusted. Given the value and deeply natural character of religious emotions, James claims, it would be disconcerting and self-destructive to hold that such feelings are intrinsically and ineluctably untrustworthy. For any philosophy which renders deceptive our deepest feelings and responses would leave us bereft of emotional, moral, and volitional investment. It would thereby disable our existence by throwing it into the category of the absurd. But any philosophy which led to such destructive consequences would itself be a practical absurdity to accept. In "The Sentiment of Rationality" James makes this point as follows:

> Now what is called "extradition" is quite as characteristic of our emotions as of our senses: both point to an object as the cause of the present feeling. What an intensely objective reference lies in fear! In like manner an enraptured man and a dreary-feeling man are not simply aware of their subjective states; if they were, the force of their feelings would all evaporate. Both believe there is outward cause why they should feel the way they do. . . . *Any philosophy which annihilates the validity of the reference by explaining away its objects or translating them into terms of no emotional pertinency, leaves the mind with little to care or act on.* (WB, 71; my emphasis)

He continues:

> Nothing could be more absurd than to hope for the definitive triumph of any philosophy which should refuse to legitimate, and to legitimate in an emphatic manner, the more powerful of our emotional and practical tendencies. (WB, 74)[19]

And again:

> No philosophy will permanently be deemed rational by all men which . . . does not . . . make a direct appeal to all those powers of our nature which we hold in highest esteem. Faith, being one of these powers, will always remain a factor not to be banished from philosophical constructions. . . . (WB, 89)

In sum, James's view is that whatever the intellectual problems which attend religious faith may be, they are ultimately less destructive—in the context of all of the aspects of a person's life—than the problems caused by the wholesale distrust of religious emotions.

James's argument is helpful in providing a pragmatic justification for trusting our religious emotions, but there are those who will object to any justification which is *merely* pragmatic. Some will claim that however morally or existentially undermining it might be to withhold trust in our religious feelings, pragmatic consequences are nevertheless not sufficient for determining whether the beliefs which those feelings generate are adequately justified. It will be argued that when we claim that our religious emotions deserve to be trusted, we mean that we have reason to think them *actually reliable*. And pragmatic reasons are irrelevant to such a claim.

Is this objection sound? Are James's arguments ultimately unpersuasive? In the first of James's arguments, as we have seen, he contends only that the fact that we have religious emotions may legitimately be used as a starting point for more fully developed justifications of religious belief.[20] In his second argument, he develops a pragmatic justification for trusting these emotions. While neither of these arguments by itself goes as far as we may like, I believe that the insights of both can be used as the basis of a more subtle argument which is also more compelling. I think, along with James, that we may reasonably use the fact that we experience religious emotions as the beginning point of an argument in support of religious conclusions. Moreover, I think James's second argument can be amplified to show not just that it is existentially or morally self-defeating to categorically deny the cognitive value of such emotions, but that it is logically self-defeating as well.

I shall begin with the modest and uncontroversial claim that a great many human beings have experienced feelings such as religious awe and wonder, and that having such feelings is an entirely normal mode of response.[21] One interesting area in which we find support for the appropriateness of the religious response is in the work of neurologist Oliver Sacks. In a recent discussion of autism, Sacks takes the position that part of the constellation of incapacities which comprise autism is the inability to have certain kinds of deep emotional and spiritual response.[22] In the report of an interview with Temple Grandin, a highly intelligent and accomplished autistic individual, Sacks asserts that despite her prodigious intellectual capacities, Ms. Grandin is incapable of a wide range of emotional, aesthetic, and spiritual feelings, including feelings of grandeur, or experiences of the numinous. Sacks recounts the following conversation with her, while they were gazing at the snow-capped Rockies:

> I asked Temple if she did not feel a sense of their sublimity. "They're pretty, yes. Sublime, I don't know." When I pressed her, she said that she was puzzled by such words, and had spent much time with a dictionary, trying

to understand them. She had looked up "sublime," "mysterious," "numinous," and "awe," but they all seemed to be defined in terms of one another.[23]

In addition to autism, Sacks also describes several other cases where frontal lobe damage left individuals incapable of affective responses such as empathy and the sense of wonder.[24]

The example of Ms. Grandin highlights the fact that we normally regard an individual as in some measure limited, as having a psychological or neurological problem, if that individual is incapable of a range of emotional response which is broad enough to include at least some sense (not necessarily theistic) of the spiritual. It is noteworthy that we share a set of criteria, reasonably well agreed upon, for what constitutes the appropriate context for religious or spiritual emotions. Moreover, just as we consider the inability of an autistic person to respond in the appropriate ways to be a deficiency, we also have a sense of what contexts would be inappropriate for engendering feelings of awe, cosmic gratitude, wonder, and the like. If a person felt awe in the presence of an ordinary kitchen appliance or a newspaper and did not explain that feeling by invoking some deeper frame of reference from which that object gained its meaning, we would judge that person's emotions to be inappropriate.

Of course the fact that religious emotions may be regarded as normal and appropriate does not by itself entail the existence of divine realities. Contrary to James's critics, however, it does help establish the probability of religious truths. Does not the fact that we can trust other healthy human functions provide presumptive evidential justification for trusting our healthy and appropriate religious feelings as well? Just as we trust that our eyes are fitted to the world (indeed, what it means to have visible property x

is for an object to look like *x* to a person with normal eyesight under normal conditions), why may we not also trust that our normal and natural religious intuitions, feelings, and experiences, are evidence for God's existence?[25] The point of the argument is this: it is irrational to hold, on the one hand, that the ability to have religious or spiritual feelings is a healthy, normal capacity, and that the inability to do so is a deficiency; and on the other hand to hold to a metaphysics and epistemology which categorically invalidates the kinds of claims which these feelings support.

It is important to emphasize that this argument, which I have developed on the basis of James's suggestions, goes beyond his specifically pragmatic argument which was discussed earlier. The conclusion here is not merely that religious feelings provide *pragmatic* justification for religious belief, but rather that they help establish the probability of religious truths—they constitute *evidence* for religious claims, in ways which even the non-pragmatist should be able to appreciate.[26] Contrary to James's critics, however, this conclusion may be reached without having to invoke the premise of pre-established harmony, or any other dubious metaphysical position.

James's support of the cognitive value of religious feelings, based on both pragmatic and non-pragmatic arguments, constitutes yet another pathway by which he has expanded the possibilities for understanding and assessing religious claims, and by which he has removed unnecessary obstacles to religious belief.

Truth in Religion

James's theory of truth, complex and often unclear, is especially puzzling in the context of his philosophy of religion. Commentators usually take it for granted that James offers a pragmatic analysis of the truth of religious claims, but there is a surprising amount of evidence to the contrary which needs to be accounted for. In opposition to his own pragmatic account of truth, there are times when James appears to advocate a realist position. In this chapter, I shall examine James's view of truth as it applies to religious claims. I shall show that in spite of the appearance of contradiction, James's account of religious truth is in fact a consistently pragmatic one. I shall also defend James against standard objections to his view, which have been widely considered to be devastating, and show how James's position is more sophisticated and convincing than his critics have supposed.

THE PRAGMATIC POSITION
AND THE CHARGE OF SUBJECTIVISM

Sooner or later almost any critical discussion of James's philosophy devolves on a series of questions concerning the issue of subjectivism. It has been a common practice to understand James's views on truth as constituting a composite metaphysical and epistemological position which, in both aspects, is judged to be inadequate. Since he holds that be-

liefs are both justified and true if they function satisfactorily in the life of the believer, critics contend that James is
committed to a pernicious subjectivism. In particular with
regard to religion, critics hold that if we were to accept a
pragmatic analysis of truth, religious claims would lose their
objective significance. While James may be more permissive
than many philosophers in his analysis of the truth and the
justification for religious belief, I shall argue that the prevailing view of him as an unregenerate subjectivist is both
simplistic and false.

If we look at James's broader philosophy, we see that
the specter of subjectivism is by no means confined to his
philosophy of religion. Many have accused James of promulgating a wanton subjectivism with regard to truth, in
whatever context it applies. James's many critics vigorously
reject his position, as presented in *Pragmatism*, that truth is
the satisfactory or good in the way of belief. In *The Pragmatic Philosophy of William James*, I have taken a position
against the critics, and shown that James believes there are
objective constraints on a belief's satisfactoriness.[1] In particular, I have held that on James's view, empirical beliefs
could not turn out to be satisfactory unless they were also
verifiable. By "verifiable," James means that the belief is progressively confirmable by experience.[2] While James's epistemological position might not go far enough to satisfy a
committed realist—who insists on the metaphysical view
that true beliefs represent facts which exist independently of
our thinking about them—nevertheless it does guarantee a
substantial degree of objectivity to truth claims.

In favor of those who interpret James as a subjectivist, it
is important to note that while he holds that verifiability
plays an indispensable role in determining the truth of empirical beliefs, the central characteristic which constitutes
the truth of a belief, for James, is that it function satisfactorily for the believer.[3] For James, empirical beliefs function

satisfactorily only on the condition that they are verifiable. But the relationship between verifiability and satisfactoriness is only a contingent one. That empirical beliefs must be verifiable in order to be satisfactory is itself merely an empirical fact about the world (albeit a critically important one), and not a conceptual truth. If it were possible for a belief to have beneficial consequences without being verifiable, its truth would not be impugned. Nothing indispensable to the *concept* of truth is lost when verifiability is eliminated.

While James holds that *empirical* beliefs must be verifiable in order to be true, there is no requirement that other true beliefs—those of a more poetic or metaphysical sort, for instance—must meet the verifiability condition. In *The Principles of Psychology*, for example, James identifies a set of propositions which he calls "postulates of rationality," whose function is not to describe an independent reality, but rather to delineate, prior to experience, the conditions any candidate description of the world must meet if it is to be intelligible. Here James does not have in mind any ordinary, narrow concept of intelligibility as restricted to semantic or syntactic adequacy. He is utilizing a rich sense of "intelligible" under which a proposition "makes sense" to us only if it satisfies our emotional, aesthetic, spiritual, as well as intellectual desires and needs. Aesthetic, moral, and spiritual postulates are distinguished from empirical claims in that they provide no basis for inferences about the natural world:

> Take those aspects of phenomena which interest you as a human being most, and class the phenomena as perfect and imperfect, as ends and means to ends, as high and low, beautiful and ugly, positive and negative, harmonious and discordant, fit and unfit, natural and unnatural, etc., and barren are all your results. In the ideal world the

kind "precious" has characteristic properties. What is precious should be preserved; unworthy things should be sacrificed for its sake; exceptions made on its account; its preciousness is a reason for other thing's actions, and the like. But none of these things need happen to your "precious" object in the real world. Call the things of nature as much as you like by sentimental, moral and aesthetic names, no natural consequences follow from the naming. (PP, 2:1259; see also ERE, 74–75)

Metaphysical principles are no less subjective:

Many of the so-called metaphysical principles are at bottom only expressions of aesthetic feeling. . . . [W]hat do all such principles express save our sense of how pleasantly our intellect would feel if it had a Nature of that sort to deal with? (PP, 2:1265)

If it is reasonable to categorize a religious belief as being a kind of spiritual postulate or metaphysical principle, then that belief is not empirical in nature, and therefore not subject to empirical tests of verifiability. If this is the case, then all that appears to be left to constitute the truth of religious beliefs, for James, is their personal satisfactoriness— the degree to which they meet the personal needs, hopes, aspirations, and desires of the believer. Of course, the fact that religious beliefs are highly personal does not mean that they must be limited or self-absorbed. Religious beliefs may help satisfy the desires for the broadest possible understanding of the meaning and purpose of existence and the foundation of moral and spiritual value. There is reason to conclude, then, that while James need not view religious beliefs as egocentric, nevertheless he does appear to endorse a profoundly subjectivistic view of the truth of religious claims.

There is no dearth of passages in which James enthusiastically reduces both the meaning and truth of religious propositions to subjective human experiences, attitudes, and actions. In *Pragmatism*, for instance, James argues that since belief in the Absolute of transcendental idealism affords comfort to a certain class of minds, it is to that degree true (P, 41).[4] In *Some Problems of Philosophy*, he claims that "'God' means that 'you can dismiss certain kinds of fear'" (SPP, 38). And one of the most frequently quoted (and misunderstood) claims in *Pragmatism*, especially popular with James's critics, is his declaration that "on pragmatistic principles, if the hypothesis of God works satisfactorily in the widest sense of the word, it is true" (P, 143).

It is understandable, then, that critics of James's theory of truth—a theory already vulnerable for its more cavalier claims against the revered canons of the philosophical establishment—have been particularly avid in their complaints about James's position on religion. The critics' response has been harsh and predictable. Bertrand Russell, for instance, claims:

> The advantage of the pragmatic method is that it decides the question of the truth of the existence of God by purely mundane arguments, namely, by the effects of belief in His existence upon our life in this world. But unfortunately this gives a merely mundane conclusion, namely, that belief in God is true, i.e. useful, whereas what religion desires is the conclusion that God exists, which pragmatism never even approaches.[5]

Sixty years later, A. J. Ayer concurs:

> The main point for James is that so long as people are psychologically able to have religious faith, and so long as it gives them emotional satisfaction, the beliefs which are its embodiment may be allowed to pass for true.[6]

And again:

> [James] strips his religious hypothesis of all pretension to give any sort of explanation of the world; it is a licence

for optimism which is in fact devoid of anything that would ordinarily be counted as religious support.[7]

He continues in this same vein:

> From the pragmatic point of view, the idea that God's in his heaven is not a justification of the claim that all is right with the world but only a more picturesque expression of it.[8]

While many scholars are not as openly dismissive as Russell and Ayer, it is common to find unfavorable comments on James's views on religious truth, even by sympathetic readers. James frequently elicits a bemused and indulgent sympathy, an acknowledgement of his engaging perspective and style, and a recognition of his importance to the American intellectual tradition. But on final analysis, many view James's philosophy of religion as essentially an unfortunate consequence of the fact that he is a pragmatist.

Let us look more closely at Russell's and Ayer's objection. Looking in particular at Russell (Ayer's claim is essentially the same), another way to put his point is that the pragmatist injunction to potential believers is self-defeating, for what it amounts to is this: "Believe that God genuinely exists" (adding, *sotto voce*, "whether He does or not") "because that is the most morally fruitful and emotionally uplifting way to deal with your experience." Russell is certainly right that a person who was struggling with the problem of religious belief would be unlikely to find this injunction the least bit helpful. Indeed, a potential believer might justifiably be offended by it. For to believe a proposition means to believe it to be true.[9] Hence, Russell's argument goes, to believe that "God exists" is to believe that " 'God exists' is true"—that "God" has objective reference, that God exists in fact. And so unless we have reason to think that God exists in fact, it is not only irresponsible, but even incoherent, to recommend that we believe in Him.

Rather than conclude that Russell has made James look foolish, however, I suggest that regardless of how ingenious his objection may appear, it actually betrays a superficial grasp of James's position. Russell rejects James's pragmatic analysis of religious truth because it contradicts his requirement that true propositions have objective reference. Since within the domains of science and common sense, we do require that true beliefs "correspond to reality" (in some uncritically examined sense of that expression), Russell appears to hold the upper hand. Russell is wrong, however, to interpret James's conception of the pragmatic truth of religion as a naive failure to acknowledge the obvious truth of realism. James's position is stronger than Russell supposes—for he is rejecting the deeper model in terms of which Russell's belief in realism is justified.

It is important to remember that based on his conception of the mind as a teleological instrument, James denies that knowing is a static copying or representational relation between the knower and the known; one which excludes consideration of the knower's purposes and interests.[10] For James, the desire to fulfill our interests provides both the motivation for cognition and the ultimate criterion of its success. Rather than being a self-justifying or intrinsically valuable activity of a disinterested intellect, rather than merely passively reflecting reality, James sees human cognition as justified by the function it fulfills in the broader biological, intellectual, psychological, moral, religious or other contexts which call it forth. There is no view of the world which is interest-neutral, James contends, and each belief has its place in a broader conceptual scheme which functions to help the individual fulfill a particular range of purposes and interests. It follows, then, that any particular claim—religious, scientific, or otherwise—is appropriately assessed only by reference to the criteria of acceptability intrinsic to the particular set of interrelated concepts and beliefs in which it functions. These criteria, in turn, will be

determined by reference to the interests which it is the
function of the conceptual scheme to fulfill.

Thus, for James, even scientific propositions, while distinct in important ways from the postulates and metaphysical principles he discusses in *The Principles*, are not mere
reflections of an independent reality. In "Reflex Action and
Theism," James gives his interpretation of physics as only
one of a possible number of conceptual schemes:

> [T]he "truths" of . . . physics . . . [are] as great an alter-
> ation and falsification of the simply "given" order of the
> world . . . as any theistic doctrine possibly can be!
>
> Physics is but one chapter in the great jugglery which
> our conceiving faculty is forever playing with the order of
> being as it presents itself to our reception. It transforms
> the unutterable dead level and continuum of the "given"
> world into an utterly unlike world of sharp differences
> and hierarchic subordinations for no other reason than to
> satisfy certain subjective passions we possess. (WB, 103)[11]

At bottom, religion and science are equally partisan:

> [Religious experiences] show the universe to be a more
> many-sided affair than any sect, even the scientific sect,
> allows for. What, in the end, are all our verifications but
> experiences that agree with more or less isolated sys-
> tems of ideas (conceptual systems) that our minds have
> framed? But why in the name of common sense need we
> assume that only one such system of ideas can be true?
> The obvious outcome of our total experience is that the
> world can be handled according to many systems of ideas,
> and is so handled by different men, and will each time
> give some characteristic kind of profit, for which he cares,
> to the handler, while at the same time some other kind
> of profit has to be omitted or postponed. . . . [S]cience
> and . . . religion are both of them genuine keys for un-

locking the world's treasure-house to him who can use either of them practically. Just as evidently neither is exhaustive or exclusive of the other's simultaneous use. (VRE, 104–5)[12]

It is interesting to note that a position much like James's was articulated by Thomas Kuhn, over a half century after James's death. Kuhn argues in support of an understanding of the practice of science in terms of the competition of alternative paradigms—accepted models or patterns of understanding—whose adequacy is measured not on the basis of how much they succeed in mirroring a preexistent reality, but rather on how well they succeed on pragmatic grounds[13] As Kuhn showed how the notion of alternative paradigms is a helpful way to understand competing ideas within science, James showed many decades earlier that such a notion is helpful in comparing and assessing the scientific enterprise as a whole with other domains such as art, religion, and philosophy. The continued influence of Kuhn's proposals, across a wide range of disciplines, provides contemporary support for the attractiveness of James's position.

Returning to Russell's criticism, we may conclude that if we accept James's pragmatic analysis, then Russell's objection is based on a false assumption. Russell believes that the "objective reference" of a proposition—which he contrasts to pragmatic adequacy—is a matter of ineluctable fact, logically independent of the consequences of believing it. But if James is right, there is no such thing as an ineluctable fact, outside of the flux of experience and independent of human interpretation. The notion of objective reference is enmeshed in language, convention, experience, and the fulfillment of human desire. Like any other concept, "objective reference" can be understood only from *within* the context of the specific constellation of beliefs, concepts, and desires in terms of which its meaning is intelligible. It follows, then, that there is no single set of independent facts (at least none which are humanly discernible) against which our claims (religious or otherwise) can be measured.

In sum, if we accept James's position, the force of Russell's objection is dissipated. Once it is understood that there can be no independently describable "objective reference" in contrast with which pragmatic adequacy is considered to fall short, Russell's critique loses whatever appearance it might have of power and irrefutability. It is a mistake to describe James as lacking an elementary understanding of objective reference. Rather, James's point is to demonstrate that that concept, as Russell understands it, is incoherent[14]

Contemporary philosophers who see themselves as within the pragmatic tradition have supported James by extending and developing a Jamesian argument. Hilary Putnam, for instance, argues that a view such as James's guarantees as much objectivity as is theoretically possible. He argues that the view which he calls "metaphysical realism"—that there is a transcendental reality which obtains independent of all actual or possible inquiry situations—is logically self-defeating. Putnam suggests that metaphysical realism be rejected in favor of "internal realism"—the position that we must hypostasize reality as a precondition for inquiry, but that that hypostasized reality has no transcendent ontological status. Putnam contends that internal realism preserves objectivity, without falling into the logical difficulties which metaphysical realism engenders.[15]

James's treatment of the concept of truth parallels his treatment of objective reference. James believes that abstracted from the contexts of its use, the concept "true" stands only in a general way for the satisfactoriness of a belief. To fully specify the meaning of truth, however, and the criteria of its applicability, it is necessary to locate the context in which the truth ascription is made.[16] As James sees it, the important issue is not about the mythical "objective reference," as Russell understands it, of particular religious claims, but rather about the appropriate paradigms under which these claims are to be understood and evaluated. Note that while we may speak of validating a proposition within a paradigm, paradigms themselves are best understood not as validated but vindicated—their acceptability is determined by how well they work to serve the purposes which engendered them.

On the most basic level, the paramount function of the scientific paradigm, by means of which its adequacy must be evaluated, is to enable us to explain events in the natural world and to predict such events in the future.[17] Religion, in contrast, contains descriptions and explanations which extend beyond the domain of the empirical—providing the believers with (putative) explanations of the moral and spiritual meaning of their lives.[18] As Ian Barbour has expressed it, "religious questions are of ultimate concern, since the meaning of one's existence is at stake. Religion asks about the final objects of a person's devotion and loyalty."[19]

This point notwithstanding, it nevertheless may be the case that some of the rules and conventions of different paradigms overlap. Indeed, it is James's belief that this is so which motivates him to look toward the possibility of a "science of religions," as we shall see in chapter 7.

THE APPARENTLY REALIST POSITION

Given the thorough and persuasive case which can be made for James's pragmatic interpretation of objective reference, it may be surprising to see that he also argues, with what seems to be equal commitment, for what appears to be a realist position regarding the truth of religious claims—one which seems to be fully consonant with a view such as Rus-

sell's and Ayer's. To my knowledge, there has been hardly
any notice in the scholarly literature, and never an explanation provided, of the numerous instances, spanning many
years, in which James makes a point of *distinguishing* the
truth of religious and metaphysical propositions from the
beneficial consequences of believing them.[20] In these passages James looks like any typical realist in holding that the
truth of any descriptive proposition—religious or otherwise—is independent of human thought, need, and desire, and can be established only on the basis of objective
evidence.

Looking first at some of his important earlier essays collected in *The Will to Believe*, we see that James takes special
pains to specify that his discussion deals *only* with the pragmatic consequences of certain religious and metaphysical
propositions, and that such consequences are *irrelevant* to
their truth. At the beginning of "Reflex Action and Theism,"
for instance, James announces that he will resist entering
into the debate about whether God actually exists, choosing instead to take up the "humbler ground," of showing that given human nature, the belief in the existence of a
theistic God—from the point of view of our psychological
and biological well-being—is the most attractive cosmo-
logical hypothesis for us to hold (WB, 93).[21] James follows a
similar strategy in "The Moral Philosopher and the Moral
Life." He argues here for the justifiability of believing in
God based on the increase in moral strenuousness which
religious commitment engenders. But he is careful to assert
that this provides only a *practical* reason to postulate God's
existence—it does not provide intellectual evidence for the
truth of religious belief. He makes it a special point to for-
bear from saying that the beneficial consequences of belief
in God constitute or provide evidence for that belief's truth
(WB, 159–62).

James's distinction, in the essays in *The Will to Believe*,
between the truth of a belief on the one hand, and the

pragmatic consequences of holding it on the other, and his choice to focus exclusively on the latter, are not limited to his discussions on religion. In "The Dilemma of Determinism," for example, James announces at the outset that he "disclaim[s] . . . all pretension to prove . . . that the freedom of the will is true" (WB, 115). Rather, he deliberately limits himself to establishing only the beneficial pragmatic consequences (specifically, the psychological and moral attractiveness) of believing in the free-will hypothesis. And even in "The Will to Believe," the essay which is most steadfastly (mis)interpreted as promulgating an undisciplined subjectivism, James seems clearly to be claiming that truth— at least scientific truth—is realistic, and is determined and discovered independently of satisfactions (WB, 26).

James's apparent anti-pragmatic realism goes beyond the articles in *The Will to Believe*. Surprisingly, in *Varieties* as well—that same book in which, as we have just seen, James so eloquently argues for the pragmatic conception of religious belief as opposed to a realist one—there are important lectures in which he appears to have fully accepted a realist perspective. Whatever else he may do in *Varieties*, James also makes it a point to *distinguish* between truth and the beneficial consequences of belief. At the end of his lectures on saintliness, for instance, while preparing his audience for his lecture on mysticism, James explains that while in his discussion of saintliness he has assessed the *consequences* of holding religious beliefs, *in contrast*, an examination of mysticism should help settle the question as to their *truth* (VRE, 300). Here he holds that pragmatic consequences of belief, however beneficial, are not sufficient to establish truth.

In Lecture XX of *Varieties* ("Conclusions"), James takes another opportunity to emphasize the distinction between the "objective truth" of religious beliefs on the one hand, and their "value for life" on the other (VRE, 401; 401 n. 23). Here he claims that the beneficial consequences of holding

religious beliefs relate to those beliefs as "purely subjective phenomena, without regard to the question of their
'truth'" (VRE, 399). In his desire to establish that a religious person's sense of a higher power is "not merely apparently, but literally true" (VRE, 403), James appears no
less a realist than Ayer or Russell in separating truth from
satisfactory consequences of belief. And he appears no less
positivistic in his insistence that empirical tests are required to determine the truth of propositions in religion.
Nor is it any accident that James's most developed defense
of this position occurs at the end of *Varieties*—where he
is setting out the requirements for a "science of religions,"
and where he is most interested in showing that science and
religion are compatible.

"The Hobgoblin of Little Minds"?

What may we conclude? Is James a pragmatist or a realist?
Given such an array of seemingly contradictory claims, how
could we possibly tell? Scholars of James are no strangers
to contradiction, but this one appears particularly intrac-
table. Is there any way to resolve, or at least explain, James's
seemingly incompatible views? Some of James's most distinguished readers have been satisfied just to accept, and even
appreciate James (as they see him) as a philosopher who did
not place a high value on consistency. George Santayana reports that "James was not consecutive, not insistent; he
turned to a subject afresh, without egotism or pedantry; he
dropped his old points, sometimes very good ones; and
he modestly looked for light from others, who had less light
than himself."[22] Similarly, Ralph Barton Perry holds that
"it would be strange if so hospitable a mind, profoundly
pluralistic both in temperament and in doctrine, had not
harbored ideas that were irrelevant or even contradictory."[23]

Perhaps we should accept the advice of Ralph Waldo Emerson, a friend of James's father, who warned that "a foolish consistency is the hobgoblin of little minds."[24] Perhaps we should enjoy James's inconsistencies as a mark of his unique—if rather eccentric—genius.

In this instance, I am less willing than others might be to accept James's apparent inconsistencies, or to believe that inconsistency in a philosopher is so easily defensible. With regard to the question of pragmatic vs. realistic interpretations of religious truth, I think that if we are sensitive to the different rhetorical circumstances in which James made his various claims, we will see that his position is, surprisingly, fully consistent.

It will help to see how James's broader intentions were different in *The Will to Believe* than they were in *Varieties*. In the lectures I have discussed in *The Will to Believe*, James's goal was not to articulate a fully worked-out philosophical system. Rather, his interest was intensely pedagogical and rhetorical. As intellectual historian George Cotkin indicates, the prevailing belief in the hegemony of science, among other things, left James's nineteenth-century audiences in need of greater moral courage and a fuller sense of spiritual meaning. From the vantage point of his role as a philosopher who was able to influence public sentiment, James offered pragmatic alternatives as appropriate options to help combat the passivity and ennui of his generation.[25]

Why, in the lectures in *The Will to Believe*, does James consider the pragmatic consequences of a belief to be distinguishable from the truth of that belief, and thereby violate one of his pragmatic axioms? I should like to offer the following as a possibility. In order successfully to challenge prevailing orthodoxies and create philosophical movement in the minds and hearts of his audiences, James was diplomatic enough to tailor his remarks to their assumptions, interests, and concerns.[26] James felt he would alienate his audiences if he approached them with a direct assault on their realist assumptions. Because he wanted to set up a context in which the members of his audience would be able to suspend their disbelief and remain receptive to his suggestions, James felt it was particularly important to refrain from flagrantly challenging their realist conception of truth. In situating his lectures by declaring that he was not addressing the issue of the *truth* of the belief in God, free will, etc., James was able to maintain his own credibility in the eyes of his audiences while at the same time convincing them of the *pragmatic* value of holding the beliefs in question.

Yet James's strategy is more wily than it appears. He grants realist assumptions, but only to show that they are ultimately *irrelevant*. James's aim was to bring the members of his audience to see for themselves that traditional (non-pragmatic) philosophical arguments for metaphysical propositions are inconclusive, and that pragmatic considerations are all that are left to circumvent the cognitive and moral gridlock which non-pragmatic methodologies produced.[27] If religious and metaphysical claims, about which it is necessary and important to take a stand, cannot be established on intellectual grounds, we are justified in using pragmatic reasons in deciding whether to believe them.[28] Having accepted the reasons to believe these propositions, any residual curiosity—as to whether these claims are *really* true—becomes merely idle, since it cannot be assuaged. The full functional significance of the claims is exhausted by a pragmatic analysis. In sum, then, using a logical strategy similar to that of "conditional proof," in the essays we have cited in *The Will to Believe*, James hypothetically accepts a realist conception of truth only in order ultimately to subvert its relevance and authority.

In the lectures in *The Will to Believe*, in his desire to help foster the moral revitalization of his audiences, James is asking them to bracket traditional philosophical and scien-

tific scruples and acknowledge the legitimacy of their religious impulses. But as I have suggested above, James's
aims in *Varieties* were different from his aims in *The Will
to Believe*, and this led him to frame his pragmatic account
differently in each case. In *The Will to Believe*, as we have
seen, James holds that religious questions are not decidable
by philosophical argument or scientific proof, and so must
be decided by reference to the value of the consequences
of the individual's belief. In *Varieties*, on the other hand,
even while arguing that religion and science represent two
distinct conceptual schemes, and acknowledging their intellectual and practical differences, James's aim is to mediate between them and show how they overlap. The overlap
occurs, James contends, in the fact that genuinely meaningful religious beliefs must be capable of empirical confirmation. And on this basis, James insists, there must be
empirical criteria for determining the truth of at least some
religious claims. We shall fully examine this position, which
James calls "piecemeal supernaturalism," in chapter 7.

   In *The Will to Believe*, James moves the focus off the issue
of the truth (as realists undertand that term) of religious beliefs, and on to the issue of the consequences of holding
those beliefs. In *Varieties*, James argues that at least some
religious claims are empirically confirmable. But it would be
a mistake to conclude, from James's change of emphasis in
Varieties, that he has thereby abandoned his pragmatism
in favor of realism.[29] For the concept of empirical confirmability, which is utilized by James in *Varieties*, is itself one
which is analyzable on pragmatic principles. This means that
it is explainable exclusively in terms of human experience.
Since it does not require reference to a world independent
of that experience, it does not involve a realist conception of
truth.[30]

   Neither of James's approaches, then, either in *The Will to
Believe* or *Varieties*, support a realist account of the truth of
religious claims. The differences between these two works is

one of James's varying emphases, *within a pragmatic analysis*, of the consequences of belief on the one hand, and their empirical confirmability on the other. My conclusion, then, is that nowhere in James's philosophy of religion is he a realist in his conception of truth.

One final question remains: If James consistently maintains his pragmatic, anti-realist position regarding the truth of religious beliefs, must we conclude that he is a subjectivist in his view of the justification of those beliefs? Does James hold, as his critics think, that any religious belief, however idiosyncratic, is justifiable, as long as it satisfies the personal desires of the believer? James does emphasize that religion is a personal matter, and he thinks it is appropriate for one's religious beliefs to incorporate elements which meet one's own unique needs (VRE, 267–68). Nevertheless, James nowhere supports superstitious or irresponsible religious belief.

James does not develop a single, unified theory of epistemic justification for religious claims; but he does provide a range of different suggestions. In *Varieties*, as we have indicated, in order to guarantee a measure of objectivity to religious claims, James introduces the condition that at least some of those claims must be capable of empirical confirmation. In *The Will to Believe,* most notably in the title essay, James appeals to a different set of criteria to ensure that religious beliefs not be held gratuitously or irresponsibly. Since I have discussed those arguments at length elsewhere,[31] I shall not repeat my discussion here. I simply note the general point that James takes pains to isolate the pragmatic and intellectual conditions which are relevant to religious belief, and with these in mind, he is able to specify, at least in general terms, the range of conditions under which such belief is justifiable. If it were James's position that religious beliefs are justified by appeal to mere subjective and whimsical satisfaction, there would have been no need for him to offer the extensively developed justifications of religion which he does offer, and which we are considering throughout this book.

To conclude our discussion, the point of this chapter has been to show that James is consistent in the maintenance of his pragmatic conception of religious truth. Moreover, I have argued that given an adequately nuanced understanding of James's conception of pragmatic truth as it applies to religion, the charge of pernicious subjectivism is insupportable and betrays a trivial understanding of his position. Finally, I conclude that even the most persuasive realist's objections to James's pragmatism underestimate the depth and incisiveness of his challenge to their position.

—— 6 ——

The Moral Significance of Religious Belief

In this chapter, I shall explore the way in which James uses pragmatic criteria to determine the moral significance of religious belief. My intention is to lay to rest a common (mis)interpretation of James, under which his pragmatic justification of religious belief is found to be crass and misguided. He is thought to appeal only to personal satisfaction, happiness, success, or other self-regarding goals in justifying religious belief. James is not without some responsibility for this less than laudable interpretation of his views. In the context of public lectures, in which he enjoys using a down-to-earth rhetoric, James speaks, for example, of religious belief as providing the believer with his "sole chance in life of getting upon the winning side" (WB, 31); of pragmatism as providing the "cash value" of ideas, religious ideas included (P, 97); and of testing meaningfulness of the attributes of God by appeal to the judgments of "us practical Americans" (P, 265).[1]

Despite statements such as these, James's primary pragmatic justification of religious belief is in fact a deeply idealistic one. As I shall show, it relies, ultimately, on an ideal of moral evolution, and on a belief in the human capacity to make significant strides in the direction of the moral perfectibility of the world.

One of the reasons James may be misunderstood stems from his use of the language of Darwinism—expressions such as "survival of the fittest" and "adaptation," for example—in his discussion of religion. In judging religious claims, James opts for "the elimination" of religious beliefs which are "humanly unfit," and "the survival" of those beliefs which are "humanly fittest" (VRE, 266). He also claims that the acceptability of religious belief depends upon the degree to which religious conduct is adaptive to environmental conditions (VRE, 287; see also 284, 298). In assessing the religious life, James uses terminology appropriate not just to biological, but also to social Darwinism. For example, (in language which obscures his true intent), he raises the possibility that the value of a person is "the utility of his function" (VRE, 297–98). And in determining the value of saintliness, James notes that "saintliness has to face the charge," which some might make, "of preserving the unfit, and breeding parasites and beggars" (VRE, 283; see also 284).

It would be natural to find James's biological, Darwinian metaphors paradoxical when used in a religious context. For such metaphors typically evoke images of struggle, violence, and domination; or at the least, the workings of blind natural forces unsupported by any spiritual foundation. The metaphors of social Darwinism, moreover, seem no more appropriate. For they suggest struggles of competition in society or the marketplace, in which spiritual motives are typically eclipsed by the desire for one's individual, social, or economic advantage.

Taken at face value, then, James's use of biological or social Darwinist metaphors in his discussion of religion suggests just the sort of crass materialism and self-absorption with which his pragmatism is frequently associated. If the Darwinist interpretation of James's religious views were correct, then it would be reasonable to reject James's characterization of the value of religion on the grounds that it excludes the most important elements of the religious life.

For to have the furtherance of one's biological, psychological, social, or economic advantage as one's primary focus, is to adopt a position which is antithetical to the religious point of view.

Indeed, it is not uncommon for religious writers to regard as inappropriate even the slightest appeal to mundane advantage as a reason in favor of religious belief. This includes even those humanistic justifications based on the personal happiness and fulfillment of the believer. Some have held that in the purest form of religious engagement, individuals must renounce themselves entirely for the sake of the acknowledgement of the divine. Even the happiness which is said to accompany spiritual renunciation may be considered problematic, if the desire for, or feeling of happiness takes greater psychological hold than the renunciation itself. Thus, writers from a wide range of religious traditions warn against "spiritual covetousness," and "the mere enjoyment of spiritual things," as ultimately undermining spiritual value.[2] They disapprove of the "constant grasping . . . for the spiritual world," and the desire for "spiritual wealth and profit."[3] They hold that if one's love of God is to be pure, one must be "not attached to it."[4]

Even if not all believers hold such a rigorous, exclusively renunciative conception of religious belief, it remains the case that living according to a religious perspective involves subordinating, to a significant degree, concerns of personal advantage and self-interest. In light of this fact, then, it would seem particularly inappropriate and insensitive for James to appeal to Darwinian criteria to justify religious belief.

I believe that to see James as a Darwinian in anything like the usual sense is to rely on only the most superficial interpretation of his claims. While it is true that James imports Darwinian language to express his views, in fact he uses the concepts of "survival," "adaptation," and "economical considerations" in novel and imaginative ways. To understand James's position, we must recognize that there is an important but unstated evaluative element in the Darwinian concepts he invokes. Consider, in particular, the concept of "adaptation." A closer look at the concept of "adaptation" will reveal that it is not a descriptive concept, as it might at first appear, but rather a normative one. It is vacuous to use "adaptation" as a criterion of success, unless one specifies the kinds of conditions to which it is *desirable* to adapt. And it is this fact which allows us to recognize the key difference between James's position and narrowly Darwinian interpretations of it. While the adaptation on which the Darwinian model relies is biological (or social, in the case of social Darwinism), for James it is not. Indeed, from James's point of view, the religious life is "adaptive" even though it is not necessarily rewarded by biological or worldly success. This is so, James thinks, because "the chief sphere of adaptation" in the religious domain is not the "seen" but the "unseen world" (VRE, 297). The operative conception of adaptation in James's discussion of religion, then, is not physical or social, but rather spiritual in character. It is for this reason that James may speak of the adaptive function of religion without having to conceive of religious belief in self-interested, and hence diminished or paradoxical terms.

James contends, for example, that "from the biological point of view, Saint Paul was a failure, because he was beheaded," but he was a success nonetheless (VRE, 299). For the success of paradigmatic religious individuals (in James's language, "saints") is to be measured not by their adaptation to *actual* physical, social, or historical conditions.[5] The *ideal* conditions are the important ones: it is to the "millennial society" that the saint is adapted—"the highest society conceivable, whether that society be concretely possible or not" (VRE, 298). As far back as 1878, in his essay "Remarks on Spencer's Definition of Mind as Correspondence," James argues against simplistic criteria of evolutionary success. In the following passage, the normative significance of the concept of "adaptation" (or as it is here called, "adjustment"), is particularly well demonstrated:

> [A] Christian, or . . . any believer in the simple creed that the deepest meaning of the world is moral . . . hold[s] that mere conformity with the outward—worldly success and survival—is not the absolute and exclusive end. In the failures to "adjust" [i.e., adapt to external conditions] . . . lies, for them, the real key to the truth—the sole mission of life being to teach that the outward actual is not the whole of being. (EPH, 17)

James makes the point more concretely, in *Varieties*, some twenty-five years later:

> [S]o far as any saint's example is a leaven of righteousness in the world, and draws it in the direction of more prevalent habits of saintliness, he is a success, no matter what his immediate bad fortune may be. (VRE, 299)[6]

If James is to be considered a Darwinist, then, it is not a biological or social Darwinism to which he is committed. It is rather a doctrine of *spiritual* Darwinism which he propounds.[7]

Indeed, throughout his philosophy of religion, James is concerned with spiritual rather than the utilitarian values which many have associated with his pragmatism. He regards the religious sensibility as our deepest source of nobility and potency (WB, 159–62, VRE, 210). Moreover, as we shall see below, he thinks that the highest possibilities of moral commitment are achievable only in the context of religious faith (VRE, 41–46, 532).

Even given the idealized scenario James envisions, however, and even if we grant his postulated moral and spiritual benefits of religious belief, we should note that he is still not so sanguine or naive as to think that religious belief is in all cases healthy or beneficial. He acknowledges that there are "horrible superstitions" which are sometimes found among believers (VRE, 386). Indeed, he goes to considerable pains to outline some of the excesses of faith—demonstrating in rich detail some of the negative consequences of religious fanaticism, excesses in purity, charity, and others (VRE, 272–95). But rather than take these shortcomings among some religious individuals as calling into question the religious life itself, James attributes them, perhaps too perfunctorily, essentially to an insufficiency of intellect.[8] And such a defect, James suggests, is at least in principle remediable.

James further strengthens his defense of religion by his observation that religion is no different from many other phenomena, in that the healthiest and deepest instances of it come surrounded by a plethora of inferior varieties. Rather than reject religion, or any other practice or form of life, on the basis of its inferior instances, James thinks that it is the better part of wisdom to acknowledge the inferior types as providing the necessary ground and context for the superior forms to arise.[9]

It is against the backdrop of James's highly idealized view of religious belief that we may best understand his support of religious faith. In his discussion of what he calls the "faith ladder," James describes a hypothetical movement of thought by which, through a series of practical decisions, one may progress to increasingly stronger religious commitment—a practical analogue to a logical *sorites*. The person at the bottom rung of James's faith ladder holds that there is "nothing absurd" in a certain religious view of the universe; the person then moves to the belief that the religious point of view "*might* have been true under certain conditions"; then progressively to the beliefs that "it *may* be true," that "it is *fit* to be true," that "it *ought* to be true," that "it *must* be true," and finally, to the commitment that "it *shall* be true, at any rate true for *me*" (SPP, 113. See also ERM, 125).

On the one hand, James does not intend the faith ladder to represent merely a psychological depiction of the way in which a person's religious belief might develop. On the other hand, however, as James is careful to point out, he does not offer the faith ladder as a description of a theoretical process of reasoning, or proof of God's existence. The importance of the faith ladder, for James, is to show, as he does more fully in his preeminent discussion of faith in "The Will to Believe," that given the nature of the conditions under which one's decisions to believe are made, one may legitimately reach conclusions regarding religious belief on the basis of practical, rather than theoretical or evidentiary processes of reasoning.[10] James holds that in thinking about God and one's place in the universe, we are justified in making the commitment to God's existence. It is this commitment which the process of moving up the faith ladder strengthens, and which its conclusion embodies. Understood in more contemporary language, the last step of the faith ladder—where the individual affirms that the proposition that God exists "*shall* be true, at any rate true for *me*"—may be considered not a descriptive claim about God, but rather a performative utterance by which the subject takes the leap and both attains and proclaims a religious commitment.[11]

James can support the process of commitment represented by the faith ladder because he departs from a prevalent view of faith, under which it is thought to be a less than desirable state, just an inadequate kind of belief, with which the subject must be satisfied in situations where adequate evidence is not available. On the contrary, James has a more proactive conception of the nature of faith: it involves making an active and morally significant choice. James believes that having faith manifests our deepest qualities of character. "It is more than probable," he claims, "that to the end of time our power of moral and volitional response to the nature of things will be the deepest organ of communication therewith we shall ever possess" (WB, 111). He sees faith as an "attitude of will" (SPP, 112), "a generous power," a "power to trust," and "the same moral quality which we call courage in practical affairs" (WB, 76; see also VRE, 353). Indeed, James regards our ability to make practical commitments—the broader category under which the adoption of faith belongs—to be our deepest personal resource, "the one strictly underived and original contribution which we make to the world" (PP, 2:1182).[12]

One reason James is willing to accept faith as the foundation for religious belief is that he thinks that on the deepest metaphysical level, reality is not logically explicable. Hence, it must be "met and dealt with by faculties more akin to our activities and heroisms and willingnesses, than to our logical powers" (EPH, 190; see also WB, 105).

While critics may regard James's support of faith as demonstrating his attraction to "the will to make-believe,"[13] they would be wrong to do so. For in fact, James qualifies his position quite carefully. He does not think that one should believe on faith in situations where it is not warranted. In particular, he thinks that faith is not appropriate when one is making judgments about a reality whose nature is determined independently of oneself, and about which it is possible to have adequate evidence (SPP, 111–13).[14]

James believes, however, that the primary issues in religion do not fall under this category. A closer look at his religious metaphysics will help us understand why. On the one hand, James does not believe in an all-powerful, all-knowing, and all-good deity who can guarantee an ultimately good outcome to the world's future.[15] On the other hand, he does not think it would be correct to predict the entropic destruction of all that we hold to be ideal.[16] Although he never adequately argues for it, James thinks of God as a finite being, who, due to His finitude, can benefit from our assistance and support. It was one of James's deepest and most abiding personal beliefs that the universe can be perfected, if we fulfill God's purposes for us by cooperating with Him in putting forth the considerable effort required to make goodness prevail.[17] But to do this, James thinks religious belief is required (WB, 160–61). Thus, James holds that to lead life religiously is "mankind's most important function" (LWJ, 2:127). He claims that "[t]o co-operate with [God's] creation by the best and rightest response seems all he wants of us. In such co-operation with his purposes . . . must lie the real meaning of our destiny" (WB, 111).[18]

However dramatic it may be to think that God actually needs human beings for the fulfillment of His moral purposes, there are occasions in which James posits an even deeper relationship between human beings and the divine. In these passages, James claims that God's very existence may be amplified by our faith and our good works. "God," he claims, "may draw vital strength and increase of very being from our fidelity" (WB, 55). In developing this more radical view, James suggests that God is most appropriately seen as not merely a *source* and *cause* of goodness. Rather, God is Himself the *embodiment* of goodness in the world.[19] Under this conception of God, religious faith takes on unusual power and poignancy. James holds that the subject's very act of believing in God, as well as the conduct which that belief generates, contribute to that same dimension of moral value of which God is the embodiment and which the subject also seeks to know.[20] Thus, James contends, since faith is such a significant formative factor in the universe, it may be justified on pragmatic grounds.

On final analysis, then, James thinks that from a pragmatic point of view, it is not the deeper spiritualization of the individual or even one's communion with the divine in itself that most deeply justifies religious belief and commitment. Rather, it is the service in God's work (or put in terms of James's more radical account, the amplification of God Himself as the embodiment of goodness) which the religious believer, through belief and action, is able to perform.[21]

As we have seen, James's pragmatic justification of religious belief depends largely on his particular conception of God: a conception which involves considerable speculation on his part, and which, at least in *Varieties*, he admits he has not established by philosophical argument.[22] Many questions about his views remain to be resolved. For example, how might God's finitude more fully be understood? In *A Pluralistic Universe*, James suggests that God is limited in power or knowledge, but he does not suggest He is limited in goodness (PU, 141). How may we best understand James's notion that God is capable of benefiting from, or even more significantly, of having his being amplified, by our help, particularly if He is not limited in goodness? And what exactly does James mean when he claims that God is an embodiment of goodness rather than its cause? What other properties may be attributed to God? In "The Will to Believe," James suggests that God has a personality (WB, 31), and in *Varieties*, he suggests that God intervenes in human affairs (VRE, 407–12). But he makes these claims while also characterizing God in another and far less specific or personal way, as a "mother sea" of experience (VRE, 543). James offers a plethora of ideas and suggestions regarding the concept of God, many of which appear to be in a state of gestation, and which require a great deal more analysis than he provides.

I should like now to focus on one issue which is particularly relevant to James's pragmatic justification of religion—the question of the relation between God and the idea of moral perfection. Let us consider the less radical of the two conceptions of God which we have described above, namely James's view that God is the source (rather than the embodiment) of goodness. As we have seen, on James's view, God is aiming toward the moral perfection of the world, and He is capable of benefiting from our help. But what might such a concept of moral perfection be like? An examination of James's views on this question will show that his position evolved in interesting ways.

James's most fully developed position on morality, which might help us to understand his idea of "perfecting the universe," is found in "The Moral Philosopher and the Moral Life." Written in 1891, it is the only essay James ever wrote on ethical theory. In "The Moral Philosopher," James argues that no particular moral value is intrinsically better than any other, and that the only viable criterion of moral value is the "satisfaction of demand." James uses the concept of "demand" to stand for the desires, interests, and ideals, of sentient beings. In "The Moral Philosopher," he is careful not to posit any substantive normative value of his own (WB, 148–49).[23] Indeed, he claims that in the end, all philosophers' normative ethical proposals are really just their own personal opinions (WB, 151). James holds that from a moral perspective, all demands are equally worthy of being satisfied.[24] Thus, he thinks the world is made better, that it moves toward an ideal of perfection, as human society progressively develops social arrangements which more and more inclusively fulfill the demands of all human beings.

God has an interesting role to play in "The Moral Philosopher." James argues, first, that we ought to posit the existence of God, since belief in Him will inspire our best moral efforts. Second, he thinks that since God is an "infinite demander,"[25] He embodies the moral arrangement which most inclusively satisfies demands.[26] As such, God's choices or judgments determine what the morally perfect world would be like. On James's scheme, then, the idea of God as the basis of morality is highly functional from a *psychological* perspective, since it generates in us a more strenuous attitude toward ethical obligation. From a *theoretical* perspective, however, God is nothing but an empty place-holder. God does not provide an explanation of, or justification for, a specific set of moral values. He is postulated as just a metaphysical foundation to support the idea that moral value is constituted by the most inclusive satisfaction of demand. Indeed, James claims that even granting that God exists, we still would be unable to discern the nature of His moral judgments: the idea of God by itself cannot provide us with any substantive moral precepts (WB, 147–50). To arrive at particular moral truths, James believes that we must rely entirely on ourselves. We can only do our best to work our way through various social arrangements, which James optimistically (if not quixotically) believes, will be progressively more inclusive in satisfying demands.

Whatever theoretical issues James's proposal involves, his normative point is clear. On the basis of the conception of perfection suggested in "The Moral Philosopher," the best way to assist God in achieving perfection would be to work toward the most inclusive possible satisfaction of demand. In "What Makes a Life Significant," written in 1898,[27] James provides a depiction, on a miniature scale, of what such inclusive satisfaction of demand might be like. He describes the Chautauqua Assembly in Chautauqua, New York, where he lectured and stayed for a week in 1896.[28] At Chautauqua, participants enjoyed classes, lectures, conferences, and entertainment. One found "sobriety and industry, intelligence and goodness, orderliness and ideality, prosperity and cheerfulness" (TT, 152). Chautauqua was a place "equipped with means for satisfying all the necessary lower and most of the superfluous higher wants of man" (TT, 152). James describes it further as follows:

> You have no zymotic diseases, no poverty, no drunkenness, no crime, no police. You have culture, you have kindness, you have cheapness, you have equality, you have the best fruits of what mankind has fought and bled and striven for under the name of civilization for centuries. You have, in short, a foretaste of what human society might be, were it all in the light, with no suffering and no dark corners. (TT, 152)

Altogether a good picture, *prima facie*, at least, of what many would envision to be a nearly perfect situation. What is interesting, however, is that James rejects the quality of life at Chautauqua as insipid—for he thinks that ultimately it discourages emotional, intellectual, and moral vitality.[29]

James's position in "What Makes a Life Significant" is particularly interesting when compared with his view in "The Moral Philosopher." As we have seen, James argues in "The Moral Philosopher" that all demands have equal moral claim to be satisfied. Yet in "What Makes a Life Significant," James rejects the life at Chautauqua, even though it approximates the ideal of the most inclusive satisfaction of demand, because such a life does not fulfill demands, or potential demands, of the morally highest sort. We see in "What Makes a Life Significant," then, a rejection of James's earlier position. In his later essay, James contends that some demands are better than others, and impose greater obligations upon us.

By the time he writes *Varieties,* James abjures entirely the earlier, normatively neutral position in "The Moral Philosopher," and he also provides a far more significant role for religious belief to play in our moral life. He depicts the most deeply religious individuals as having the most profound moral principles and motives. He describes them as prepared to sacrifice their lower desires for the sake of higher values, inspired by their belief in God and their desire to assist Him morally.[30] Unfortunately, James never solves the problem he identifies in "The Moral Philosopher": he never tells us how religious believers may be justified in claiming to know what God's desires are. Nevertheless, he feels confident that moral perfectibility lies in the fulfillment of religious, indeed, judging by his examples, characteristically Christian ideals.

James contends, for example, that the saintly individual demonstrates "severity for one's self, accompanied with tenderness for others" (VRE, 211). Saints feel that they are in "a wider life than that of this world's selfish little interests" (VRE, 219). The saint rejects his or her "own inferior self and its pet softnesses" (VRE, 214). James continues:

> [A saintly person's feelings keep him] immune against infection from the entire groveling portion of his nature. Magnanimities once impossible are now easy; paltry conventionalities and mean incentives once tyrannical hold no sway. (VRE, 216)

Finally, if we take "the present world's arrangements" to which James refers in the following passage as equivalent to the mechanisms we have in place for the inclusive satisfaction of demand, we can see how far James's religious ethics transcends his earlier, non-religious ethical theory. In describing the saintly individual, James asserts the following:

> [I]f radically followed, [the precept "love your enemies"] would involve such a breach with our instinctive springs of action as a whole, and with the present world's arrangements, that a critical point would be practically passed, and we should be born into another kingdom of being. Religious emotion makes us feel that other kingdom to be close at hand, within our reach. (VRE, 229)

We have seen, then, that James's thinking about ethics evolved over time. In "The Moral Philosopher" he argues for the view that all demands are morally equivalent. His conception of the ideal moral universe, as one in which all demands are inclusively satisfied, has certain strengths.[31] It may even be regarded as in some ways reminiscent of Kant's ethical position,[32] in that on both James's and Kant's views (if for different reasons), claims to moral value must be universalizable. On the model of moral perfection in "The Moral Philosopher," James may be seen to be proposing, in a Kantian vein, that where moral value is constituted by the most inclusive satisfaction of demand, each individual should legislate for oneself only what one is capable of legislating for all human beings. Whatever the advantages of his view in "The Moral Philosopher," however, James goes beyond it in *Varieties*. Ultimately, James's moral ideal is not the inclusive satisfaction of any and all demands, but rather the achievement of religiously inspired self-sacrifice. In working to help God perfect the universe, we elevate the nature of our demands, as well as the actions which follow upon them. In so doing, we elevate that part of God's creation for which we are most directly responsible. For James, then, the ultimate pragmatic criterion of the value of religious belief is the progressive perfection of the individual in that individual's attempt to contribute to the perfection of the world.

To summarize our discussion in this chapter, we have found that the pinnacle of James's religious landscape, and his ultimate justification of religious belief, is simultaneously ethical and pragmatic. It is his vision of the believer, working together with God, toward the moral perfection of the universe. The sense of "pragmatic" which is here being invoked is, of course, one which would be unrecognizable to those accustomed to its popular narrow and pejorative meaning. But the point of this chapter has been to show that the fact that "pragmatic" reasons may be so highly idealized serves only to demonstrate the depth and breadth of James's pragmatism. Whatever the particular difficulties of James's theory, it remains true that his pragmatic principles, when properly understood, provide him with a rich and idealistic vision of the value of religious belief.

It is a long way from James's vision of the religiously inspired moral life to a fully articulated justification of his position. But given James's own obvious commitment to the religious values he endorses, there is one added dimension of *Varieties* which is noteworthy. In light of his view that we have an obligation to help perfect the universe, might not James have regarded writing *Varieties* as his own contribution toward that very end? If James could stimulate others to adopt the religious and ethical perspective he describes with such intensity, or even lead them to consider more deeply the issues involved, would not he himself have contributed, in some measure, toward his postulated ideal of the moral perfection of the world?[33] Perhaps this explains James's two assertions, one made lightly—that he was "heaven's champion";[34] and the other, made seriously—that writing *Varieties* was his own religious act (LWJ, 2:127).

We turn now to a fuller examination of James's religious metaphysics, and to the way in which he deals with the thorny problems of establishing a scientific basis for religious belief.

—— 7 ——

The Empirical Implications
of God's Existence

I

We have seen in chapter 2 that James holds the view that religious belief enables a person to understand the world in a new light. The religious believer sees ordinary events as imbued with religious significance. But while James argues for the importance of seeing the world in religious terms, by the time he concludes *Varieties*, he comes to believe that this interpretive function of religious beliefs is not sufficient to justify them. Religious claims, he argues, should also be "genuine scientific hypothes[es]" (VRE, 407). That means, for James, that they must have genuine consequences in the natural world.

In the "Conclusions" and "Postscript" to *Varieties*, James argues against those who hold a view which he calls "universalistic supernaturalism" (VRE, 409).[1] On this view, as he describes it:

[T]he world of the ideal has no efficient causality, and never bursts into the world of phenomena at particular points. The ideal world, for them, is not a world of facts, but only of the meaning of facts; it is a point of view for judging facts. . . . It cannot get down to the flat level of experience and interpolate itself piecemeal between distinct portions of nature, as those who believe, for example, in divine aid coming in response to prayer, are bound to think it must. (VRE, 410)[2]

Thus, the universalistic supernaturalist believes that God is an abiding presence, but one whose existence has no particular implications for the empirical world. Arguing against this position, James claims resolutely that however important it is to discern religious meaning in what we observe, to restrict religion merely to the level of meanings is to trivialize it. Putting his point another way, James claims that universalistic supernaturalism "surrenders . . . too easily to naturalism" (VRE, 410). He thinks that a God from whose existence we can infer no particular empirical consequences is otiose: a God without effects in the world of our experience is pragmatically equivalent to no God at all.

James contrasts the view that God has no effect on our experience with his own position, which he calls "piecemeal supernaturalism." He uses this name to indicate that, in his judgment, in order for the hypothesis of God's existence to be meaningful, it must entail some set of particular ("piecemeal") differences in the empirical world. The hypothesis of piecemeal supernaturalism, James claims, supports "the instinctive belief of mankind" that "God is real since he produces real effects" (VRE, 407).[3] What this means for James is the following:

> [R]eligion . . . is not a mere illumination of facts already elsewhere given, not a mere passion, like love, which views things in a rosier light. It is indeed that, as we have seen abundantly. But it is something more, namely, a postulator of new facts as well. The world interpreted religiously . . . must have . . . a natural constitution different at some point from that which a materialistic world would have. (VRE, 407–8; see also 411)

As the first step in finding the empirical implications of religious claims, James thinks that we must eliminate irrelevant aspects of the varying religious beliefs which people hold. James recognizes the problem presented by religious pluralism: that the various religions make claims which are inconsistent with one another, while each in turn nevertheless claims to be in possession of the truth. More importantly, he recognizes that the particular doctrines of any given religion are often "absurd or incongruous" when examined from a scientific point of view (VRE, 359).[4]

In light of these difficulties, James believes that as a philosopher, his role is not to engage in theological speculation, but rather to provide analysis and criticism (VRE, 359, 397).[5] In particular, James sees his responsibility to be that of providing a way to formulate a "science of religions" (VRE, 359–60, 404–5). His goal is to understand religion in a way which avoids the scientific and philosophical difficulties to which the varying religions are typically prone. As a chemist would pour a liquid through a filter to leave the impurities behind, James's objective is to filter out the sectarian and intellectually problematic aspects of each religion, those beliefs which are merely local and accidental functions of historical conditions, so that he may identify and assess the essential characteristics which they all share. At the conclusion of *Varieties*, James claims that he can show that once religion is understood in terms of its essential characteristics, its claims are capable of empirical confirmation. And for James, this means that religion is compatible with the methods and principles of empirical science.

But how is it possible to achieve such a remarkable goal? How exactly does James go about attempting this, and what is his level of success? His first step is to identify a set of three propositions he believes can be extracted from specific religious creeds—propositions which he thinks constitute the nucleus of all religions:

> Summing up in the broadest possible way the characteristics of the religious life . . . it includes the following beliefs:

1. That the visible world is part of a more spiritual universe from which it draws its chief significance;

2. That the union or harmonious relation with that higher universe is our true end.

3. That prayer or inner communion with the spirit thereof—be that spirit "God" or "law"—is a process wherein work is really done, and spiritual energy flows in and produces effects, either psychological or material, within the phenomenal world. (VRE, 382)[6]

Even if we grant James his contention that these propositions capture the essence of all religions, we may still wonder whether they help him to any degree in his program of establishing religious propositions as empirically confirmable. James focuses on the third proposition on his list as the most promising candidate by which the empirical confirmation of religion is made possible. This would seem to be a good choice on his part, since the first two propositions, which address issues of meaning and purpose, are normative rather than empirical. Hence they are not appropriate candidates for empirical confirmation.

In the third proposition, James identifies prayer as the phenomenon by means of which religious propositions may be confirmed. "The genuineness of religion," he claims, "is indissolubly bound up with the question whether the prayerful consciousness be or be not deceitful" (VRE, 367). "Prayer" is defined rather broadly by James. In prayer, he holds, one feels oneself to be in an interactive, transactional relationship with the divine (VRE, 366–67). Prayer, he contends, is "every kind of inward *communion* or *conversation* with the power recognized as divine" (VRE, 365; my emphasis).

Communion is the element which is most important in James's conception of prayer, and we shall turn to a discussion of it shortly. However, some of what James has to say about prayer on the model of a *conversation* between the subject and what that individual takes to be the divine will help give us a fuller picture of his overall view on the matter.

With regard to prayer understood as a discursive phenomenon, as a form of conversation with the divine, we may note that there are certain forms of prayer which James chooses at the outset to exclude from his analysis. One of these is formal prayer, viz., a recitation, typically using preset formulae, which is primarily ritualistic or performative in character (VRE, 365–66). The unsuitability of formal prayer, for appreciating the dimension of religion which interests James, lies in the fact that the meaning of a formal prayer is understandable only by reference to the institutionalized religion in which it functions.[7] James does not go so far as to deny that there may be some religious emotions and states of mind which are best achieved within the specific formal contexts in which they are nurtured. Nevertheless, since his aim is to understand religion solely as a personal, spiritual phenomenon, he wants to factor out what he regards as irrelevant, if not sometimes spiritually inhibiting, institutional accouterments (VRE, 32–33, 173).

In addition, in response to those who might think of prayer solely as a means of petitioning God, James makes it a point to acknowledge that prayer extends beyond its petitional forms. He is right to do so, since there are, of course, many kinds of prayer beyond petitional ones. They include, for example, prayers of meditation, praise, suffering, adoration, relinquishment, gratitude, and surrender, to name a few.[8]

It is prayer as communion which holds the central place in James's analysis of the confirmation of religious claims. One interesting aspect of James's broad conception of prayer as communion is that for him, prayers need not be addressed to a particular divine being. Indeed, prayers need not be "addressed" at all. To pray, for James, it is not necessary to engage in a particular performance, or verbalize certain propositions, even silently in one's mind. A person's sense of a consecrated dimension of existence would appropriately count as prayer, for James, as long as that person sees him or herself as being in transaction with the divine. Moreover, given his definition of prayer as including all forms of communion with the divine, James is able to include both mystical and conversion experiences within the category of prayer.[9] Indeed, insofar as mystical experiences are held to embody the deepest level of divine communion, they are the consummation and archetype of prayer.

In James's hands the concept of prayer, understood as the experience of communion, is a highly inclusive one,[10] and it invites the following question: How, exactly, may experiences of communion provide empirical confirmation of the claims of religion? James's answer is as follows: In communion, one regards oneself as having come in contact with an exterior helping power:

> The appearance is that in [communion] something ideal, which in one sense is part of ourselves and in another sense is not ourselves, actually exerts an influence, raises our centre of personal energy, and produces regenerative effects unattainable in other ways. . . . At these places, at least, I say, it would seem as though transmundane energies, God, if you will, produced immediate effects within the natural world to which the rest of our experience belongs. (VRE, 412)

In another passage, James makes the same point in terms of the continuity between the individual and the divine consciousness:

> [In communion, the subject] becomes conscious that this higher part is conterminous and continuous with a *more* of the same quality, which is operative in the universe outside of him, and which he can keep in working touch with. . . . (VRE, 400)[11]

But what is this "more," this exterior helping power, these transmundane energies, and how do they explain the effects which James believes only prayer can achieve? James is unusually restrained at this juncture, for he realizes the importance of maintaining his credibility with his scientifically-oriented listeners and readers, whose minds he is trying to open to the possibility of accepting religious belief. No less importantly, James is trying to keep faith with the empirical scientist in himself. Thus, in the case of communion, when it comes to specifying exactly what it is that produces regenerative effects in the believer, James allows, at least tentatively, for the possibility of a purely naturalistic explanation. It may be the case, James claims, that the vitalization and re-energizing of life which occur as a result of communion derive from a merely subjective, psychological source, and as such, can be explained without appeal to the existence of an independent, divine power.[12] James holds, then, that *conservatively* interpreted, the putative higher powers which are posited as continuous with the individual may be entirely subjective; located merely in the "subconscious" (he also calls it the "transmarginal," or "subliminal") region of the individual's own mind:

> [W]hatever it may be on its *farther* side, the "more" with which in religious experience we feel ourselves connected is on its *hither* side the subconscious continuation of our conscious life. Starting thus with a recognized psychological fact as our basis, we seem to preserve a contact with "science" which the ordinary theologian lacks. At the same time the theologian's contention that the religious man is moved by an external power is vindicated, for one of the peculiarities of invasions from the subconscious region is that they take on objective appearances, and suggest to the Subject an external control. In the religious life the control is felt as "higher"; but since on our hypothesis it is primarily the higher faculties of our own hidden mind

which are controlling, the sense of union with the power beyond us is a sense of something, not merely apparently, but literally true. (VRE, 403)[13]

Far from being supernatural, then, this "transmarginal," "subliminal," or "subconscious" region of the individual's mind to which James refers may be a purely natural phenomenon, and hence it is nothing to which, on the face of it, the empirical scientist would have reason to object. Indeed, James counts it as a point in favor of his theory that "[t]he *subconscious self* is nowadays a well-accredited psychological entity" (VRE, 402).[14] James therefore feels confident that he has achieved the critical step toward a science of religions when he concludes that if the religious hypothesis—namely, that "the conscious person is continuous with a wider self through which saving experiences come"—is understood as a strictly empirical one, then it is "literally and objectively true as far as it goes" (VRE, 405; emphasis removed). In sum, then, if James were asked the question "What is the seemingly higher power with which the subject is in communion in religious experience?" his initial and conservative reply would be that it may be nothing more than the subject's own subconscious mind.[15]

It is hard to imagine a more disappointing answer. To suggest that it may be no more than the deeper regions of the individual's own mind which provide the source and sufficient explanation of our religious sensibility is to abandon entirely the religious point of view. If this were all there were to James's proposal, we would have to conclude that he has paid an impossibly high price in his attempt to mediate between science and religion. Indeed, it would not be too much to say, based on what we have seen thus far, that on James's account, the question of the empirical confirmation of religious belief is entirely vitiated. For on the present proposal, there is nothing divine remaining which would need to be confirmed.

But James's conception of science was not so restricted that he failed to appreciate the paucity of this initial proposal. Indeed, having tried to satisfy the more narrowly scientifically-oriented members of his audience, James prepares to move beyond his original, conservative conclusion. He hopes to use the subconscious mind not as the final word in his philosophy of religion, but rather as a secure starting point from which to generate a more ambitious, if more tentative, hypothesis (VRE, 399–408). In suggesting his richer proposal, James proceeds with great caution, for he realizes he is entering into territory towards which many of his readers and listeners have considerable resistance. Indeed, James is so unsure of his reception, and perhaps even of his own confidence in his position, that, although he presents his hypothesis as a scientifically respectable one, he also asserts that it is merely his own "over-belief," that is to say, his own personal opinion (VRE, 405).

James's hypothesis is that religious experiences do not come so much *from* the subconscious mind as they do *through* it: the subconscious is a doorway through which experiences of the divine may enter into conscious awareness. This is possible, James holds, because the divine reality is itself an objectively existing higher level of consciousness, in which we all participate. James's proposal, which he offers in a hypothetical tone, is as follows:

> But just as our primary wide-awake consciousness throws open our senses to the touch of things material, so it is logically conceivable that *if there be* higher spiritual agencies that can directly touch us, the psychological condition of their doing so *might be* our possession of a subconscious region which alone should yield access to them. The hubbub of the waking life might close a door which

in the dreamy Subliminal might remain ajar or open. (VRE, 197)[16]

In setting forth the hypothesis of the objective existence of the divine,[17] as known through the medium of the subconscious mind, James clearly avoids the deflatingly reductionistic character of his previous suggestion—that the divine may be nothing more than the individual's own subconscious mind. Nevertheless, the question now arises as to whether James has moved too far in the opposite direction. On the one hand, as we have seen, personal experiences deriving from the subconscious are clearly insufficient as a surrogate for God. Yet on the other hand, it seems far too great a leap to infer the existence of an objective, independent divinity solely from the occurrence of such subjective experiences. One initially plausible objection to James's philosophy of religion, then, is that in basing his theological claims upon the individual's subjective experience, he seems to have consigned himself to achieving either too little or too much. Insofar as we think of James's view in terms of subjective states on the one hand and the objective facticity of the divine on the other, we are bound to think that he has failed. Indeed, James may have had something like this objection in mind when, while preparing the Gifford lectures, (and utilizing, as was then current, a broad conception of biology as including psychology), he predicted that they would be "too biological for the religious, [and] too religious for the biologists" (VRE, 545).[18]

Before we accept such a negative conclusion, however, we should note that the claim that James has tried to achieve too little, as well as the claim that he has tried to achieve too much, both share the same unquestioned assumption. Both presuppose that if God exists, the relationship between human beings and the divine is a relationship between two metaphysically distinct entities. For it is only on this assumption that one would feel compelled to deny both the claim that God is reducible to the individual's subjective states, as well as the claim that the individual's subjective states may justify the inference that God exists. But James does not share the assumption of this metaphysical dualism. While he does not think that God is reducible to our own subconscious states, at the same time he denies that God is metaphysically distinct from human beings (or for that matter, other existents). What this means for our discussion thus far is the following: if James were correct in his metaphysical position, then whatever epistemological problems might be entailed by the subject's claim to be in genuine contact with a divine being, they would not include the problem of how, cognitively, to leap from one metaphysical domain (subjective states) to another entirely distinct one (independent divine reality). For given James's denial of a dualism between human beings and God, no such leap is required.

James's view that there is no metaphysical separation between human beings and the universal divine consciousness is a rich and controversial one.[19] While James most fully develops his position in *A Pluralistic Universe*,[20] he lays the foundations for it in *Essays in Radical Empiricism*, and also much earlier, in *The Principles of Psychology*. The beginning-point of James's formulation is his notion of the self. James rejects the view of the self as a substantive entity. Rather, he thinks that personal identity is always in flux—the self is an ever-changing series of experiences. As a series of experiences, the boundaries of the self are constantly changing. Since, for James, God himself is just a wider series of experiences, and since, as series of experiences, individuals have no set boundaries between them (as there would be on a substantive view of the self), the metaphysical foundation is set for defending the continuity of the personal and the divine consciousness. In the following passages in *A Pluralistic*

Universe, James refers to the divine consciousness as "a more really central self in things," and suggests the way in which the continuity between the personal and the divine self is possible:

> My present field of consciousness is a centre surrounded by a fringe that shades insensibly into a subconscious more. . . . What we conceptually identify ourselves with and say we are thinking of at any time is the centre; but our *full* self is the whole field, with . . . indefinitely radiating subconscious possibilities of increase. . . . (PU, 130)

He continues:

> Every bit of us at every moment is part and parcel of a wider self. . . . And just as we are co-conscious with our own momentary margin, may not we ourselves form the margin of some more really central self in things which is co-conscious with the whole of us? May not you and I be confluent in a higher consciousness, and confluently active there, tho we now know it not? (PU, 131)[21]

Thus we see that James's view—that there is no epistemic leap required between the subconscious mind and God—is based on his religious metaphysics, which unites the subconscious and the divine fields of experience.

Whatever we may make of the adequacy of James's metaphysical views, the point to note here is that if his position on religious metaphysics is assumed, his religious epistemology is rendered more persuasive. If his metaphysical views are accepted, then there is at least no immediate basis for the charge that James concludes too much in making claims about a divine reality on the basis of religious experience. It is important to note, however, that even if we do not accept James's religious metaphysics, we need not reject the evidentiary value of experiences of communion. As we have seen in chapters 3 and 4, James offers a number of arguments which support, either directly or indirectly, the veridicality of experiences of communion, arguments which do not necessarily depend upon acceptance of his particular metaphysical position.

II

We have seen that James regards the experience of religious communion to be a central element in the empirical confirmation of religious claims. But is the experience of communion sufficient to put religion on a scientific basis? James's answer to this question is by no means univocal. As we have seen above, the central point of the view James calls "piecemeal supernaturalism," to which he subscribes, is the claim that if religious propositions are to be meaningful, they must entail empirical consequences. And indeed, not just any empirical consequences will count as adequate for James. They must be consequences in the natural world, over and above the believer's experiences of communion. For if such consequences are not implied in religious claims, James believes, the concept of God will "fall short" of being a genuine scientific hypothesis. The following passage is important as an illustration of the way in which James rejects, as unscientific, the view of God which restricts the empirical consequences of His existence solely to the subject's personal religious experience:

> A good hypothesis in science must have other properties than those of the phenomenon it is immediately invoked to explain, otherwise it is not prolific enough. God, meaning only what enters into the religious man's experience of union, falls short of being an hypothesis of this more useful order. (VRE, 407)

What, then, are the wider-ranging empirical consequences which we seek? It is interesting that in further elaborating the position of piecemeal supernaturalism, James offers as examples of empirical consequences of God's existence only those phenomena in which *other* "piecemeal supernaturalists" believe. James asserts that "common men" believe, for example, in "miracles and providential leadings" (VRE, 409), and "divine aid coming in response to prayer" (VRE, 410; see also 408). But when James sets out his own version of piecemeal supernaturalism, he is less willing to commit himself. While James stands firm in his view that the hypothesis of God's existence must have *some* empirical consequences beyond that of the subject's sense of communion, nevertheless there are no additional consequences about which he feels fully confident. He can give only his own personal assurances that they exist, but he cannot be more specific. Using the terms "faith state" and "prayer state" to stand for religious communion, James asserts his position as follows:

> What the more characteristically divine facts are, apart from the actual inflow of energy in the faith-state and the prayer-state, I know not. But the over-belief on which I am ready to make my personal venture is that they exist. (VRE, 408)

In the following passage, James once again expresses his inability to come up with further empirical consequences of God's existence:

> If asked just where the differences in fact which are due to God's existence come in, I should have to say that in general I have no hypothesis to offer beyond what the phenomenon of "prayerful communion" . . . immediately suggests. (VRE, 411–12)

The situation in which James finds himself, then, in attempting to establish a science of religions, is that of insisting that there are certain phenomena which are required for the empirical confirmation of religious belief, but at the same time, being unable to specify any examples of them.

What can we make of such an anomalous situation? James finds himself in this uncomfortable position, I suggest, because, with regard to their empirical consequences, he is asking too much of religious claims. It is clearly understandable, in light of his general philosophical principles, that James desires to establish that at least some religious claims are capable of empirical confirmation.[22] Nevertheless, I would suggest that James's attempt to show that religion is "scientific," is misguided, if that means that religious propositions are expected to entail a particular set of events in the physical world, over and above the communion experiences of believers.

In my judgment, James ought to have been satisfied with the subject's sense of communion as providing empirical support for religious belief. For to require further empirical support for religious belief is essentially to look in the wrong place. It is to fail to understand the degree to which religion is a personal phenomenon. Let us recall that James defines religion, for the purposes of his study in *Varieties*, as "the feelings, acts, and experiences of individual men in their solitude, so far as they apprehend themselves to stand in relation to whatever they may consider the divine" (VRE, 34; emphasis removed). This definition, I suggest, is not an arbitrarily chosen one, or simply one which James decides upon due to his interest in psychology. Rather, the definition captures, I believe, one of the most fundamental characteristics of religion, at least Judeo-Christian religion, namely, the personal relationship, as manifested in experiences of communion, between the subject and what that subject regards as the divine. To claim that there must be empirical confirmation of the propositions of religion, beyond experiences of religious communion, is not to strengthen religion, but rather to diminish the significance of the per-

sonal relationship in which religious individuals understand
themselves to be participating.

III

It is interesting to note that even in the midst of James's attempt to show that religious claims must have implications
for the empirical world over and above the experiences of
communion, he is groping toward a deeper position. This
is best demonstrated in "Reason and Faith," a brief and
little-known but trenchant essay written several years after
Varieties.[23] In trying to identify the particular empirical
difference which the existence of God may make, James
brings to light one particular kind of experience of religious
communion. The experience he describes involves "new
ranges of life succeeding on our most despairing moments"
(ERM, 128). James points to cases in which the subject
feels, from out of the depths of despair, a renewal of energy
and hope, which, James believes, cannot adequately be explained in non-religious terms:

> [These experiences are] *discontinuous with 'natural' ex-*
> *perience, and invert its values.* But as they come and are
> given, Creation widens to our view. *They suggest that our*
> *'natural' experience, so-called, may only be a fragment of re-*
> *ality.* (ERM, 128; my emphasis)

James further develops this position in the following passage. Here it is clear that he has abandoned his contention that religious beliefs must have empirical consequences
over and above the believer's experience of communion.
Indeed, James goes so far as to suggest that religious facts
may *contradict* the facts of nature as we know them:

> There are resources in us that naturalism with its literal
> and legal virtues never recks of, possibilities that take our

breath away, and show *a world wider than* either *physics or philistine ethics can imagine.* Here is a world in which all is well, *in spite* of certain forms of death, indeed *because* of certain forms of death, death of hope, death of strength, death of responsibility, of fear and worry, death of everything that paganism, naturalism and legalism pin their trust on. (ERM, 128)[24]

The passages I have cited reveal a subtle and profound shift in James's approach to the question of the confirmation of religious belief. In these passages, James alludes to some of the regenerative spiritual experiences which satisfy his requirement, in establishing a science of religions, that empirical implications follow from the proposition that God exists. But it is these very same experiences, according to James, which call into question the relevance of other sorts of empirical facts in the religious context. In the passage above, James makes it a point to distinguish between religious experiences and ordinary sensory experiences. Moreover, in the same essay in which this passage appears, he claims that naturalistic science by itself, based on ordinary sensible experience, will yield only non-religious conclusions (ERM, 127). It would have been a minute step, *at most*, for the earlier James, of *Varieties*, who hoped to establish a science of religions, to see that for religious propositions to be meaningful, it is not necessary to be able to use them to predict a specific set of occurrences in the physical world. For religious claims to be meaningful, as James recognizes in "Reason and Faith," all that is required is that, through the medium of experiences of communion, there be a religious *dimension* of the world which is discernible by individuals of religious sensibility. If I am correct that it is misguided to require that the implications of religious propositions be anything more than the experiences gained by religious communion, then James would have been more successful had he more wholeheartedly adopted, from the outset, the position he was reaching toward in "Reason and Faith." Indeed, in retrospect, one may see those passages in *Varieties*, in which James argues that religion and science constitute alternative paradigms, to be earlier intimations of this later position.[25]

Looking at the issue we have been considering in light of the position James more fully develops in his later—and in my judgment, deeper—work, the result is this: If personal experiences of religious communion may be used to negate claims about the natural world, perhaps the best reply James could have made to the question "Can there be a science of religions?" would have been, "Happily, there cannot."

Before ending with a conclusion which is so antithetical to James's attempt to establish a science of religions, one final point is worth noting. James was always experimenting philosophically; indeed, sometimes at a pace even faster than he himself could sustain. In *Varieties*, James sometimes challenges the very conception of science which he himself utilizes when he tries to show, in that same book, that a science of religions is possible. In the following passage, James argues for an enriched conception of science, claiming that science is more like religion than religion's critics have supposed:

> [T]he divorce between scientist facts and religious facts may not necessarily be as eternal as it at first sight seems, nor the personalism and romanticism of the world . . . be matters so irrevocably outgrown. The final human opinion may . . . revert to the more personal style. . . . If this were so, the rigorously impersonal view of science might one day appear as having been a temporarily useful eccentricity rather than the definitively triumphant position which the sectarian scientist at present so confidently announces it to be. (VRE, 395 n. 2)[26]

In sum, then, the answer to the question of whether James has successfully reconciled science and religion turns out to be far more complicated than it first appears. When James tries to show that religion may meet the demands of science, he sets up standards which he himself can find no real way to meet. He has failed to substantiate his own claim that religious propositions have and must have empirical consequences outside the believer's experience of communion. But he has also provided, in "Reason and Faith," the foundation for an enriched religious epistemology under which the call for such consequences is not only unnecessary, but also inappropriate. Finally, James has raised the question of what the appropriate conception of science might be. He proposes that it is not simply the case that religion must meet the requirements of science, but also, in a suggestive but not yet fully articulated way, that science must meet the requirements of religion.

Notes

1. Introduction

1. Letter to Henry W. Rankin, LWJ, 2:58.
2. Hereafter referred to as *Varieties*.
3. Reprinted as Appendix I of *Pragmatism*. See especially 258–60.
4. Both John E. Smith, in his "Introduction" to *Varieties* (xiii), and H. S. Thayer, in his "Introduction" to *Pragmatism* (xxvii n. 47), find this fact significant enough to mention.
5. See especially Lectures VII and VIII.
6. LWJ, 2:76–77; "A Suggestion about Mysticism," EPH, 157–64. For a discussion of James's nitrous oxide experiences, see WB, 217–21; VRE, 307–8.
7. See also VRE, 410. We shall see in chapter 7 that James's rejection of Christianity is not in itself quite as significant as it may seem, since he believes that all religious creeds are merely contingent overlays on the essence of religion.
8. See Henry Samuel Levinson, *The Religious Investigations of William James* (Chapel Hill: University of North Carolina Press, 1981), 26.
9. See especially James's famous distinction between the "tender-minded" and "tough-minded" (P, 13).
10. See VRE, 66–67, 344–45. An incident in the life of C. S. Lewis provides an interesting anecdote in this context. In his biography of Lewis, A. N. Wilson chronicles a debate between Lewis and Elizabeth Anscombe at the Socratic Club at Oxford in 1948, concerning Lewis's arguments for the existence of God (*C.S. Lewis* [New York: W. W. Norton & Company, 1990],

213–14). As Wilson describes the event, Lewis was "thoroughly trounced" by Anscombe. Afterwards, Lewis reported to an acquaintance that "his argument for the existence of God had been demolished." As Faith McNulty notes, however, in a review of Wilson's book, Lewis did not therefore cease to believe (*New Yorker,* 26 November 1990, 131).

The problem which confronted Lewis is addressed directly by Alvin Plantinga. In showing what he takes to be the strengths of Calvin's rejection of natural theology (i.e., the provision of reasons and arguments for God's existence), Plantinga supports Calvin's view that religious faith which is based on argument is likely to be "unstable and wavering," the "subject of perpetual doubt." Plantinga continues:

> If my belief in God is based on argument, then if I am to be properly rational, epistemically responsible, I shall have to keep checking the philosophical journals to see whether, say, Anthony Flew has finally come up with a good objection to my favorite argument. This could be bothersome and time-consuming; and what do I do if someone does find a flaw in my argument? Stop going to church? ("Reason and Belief in God," in *Faith and Rationality: Reason and Belief in God,* ed. Alvin Plantinga and Nicholas Wolterstorff [Notre Dame, Ind.: University of Notre Dame Press, 1983], 67)

11. See VRE, Lecture XVIII. See also James's claim, in *The Meaning of Truth,* that the appeal of religious (and other) world views is "to our whole nature's loyalty and not to any emaciated faculty of syllogistic proof" (MT, 139).

12. His second aim, a subject which shall be discussed in chapter 6, was this:

> [T]o make the hearer or reader believe, what I myself invincibly do believe, that, although all the special manifestations of religion may have been absurd (I means its creeds and theories), yet the life of it as a whole is mankind's most important function. (LWJ, 2:127).

13. For a good discussion of James's historical and cultural context, see George Cotkin, *William James, Public Philosopher* (Baltimore: Johns Hopkins University Press, 1990), especially

chapter 4. For a broader discussion of the responses by James, Peirce, and Dewey to the cultural implications of scientific method, see David A. Hollinger, "The Problem of Pragmatism in American History," in *In the American Province* (Bloomington: Indiana University Press, 1985).

14. See, for example, WB, 49–50, for James's discussion of this aspect of the scientific rationalist's position.

15. For James's discussion of the problems of reductionism (he calls it "medical materialism"), see VRE, Lecture I. For an example of psychological reductionism, see Sigmund Freud, *Totem and Taboo*, trans. A. A. Brill (New York: Moffat, Yard and Company, 1918) and *The Future of an Illusion*, trans. W. D. Robson-Scott (New York: Liveright Publishing Corporation, 1955). For sociological reductionism, see Emile Durkheim, *The Elementary Forms of the Religious Life*, trans. Joseph Ward Swain (London: George Allen and Unwin, 1957). For an incisive discussion of Freud and Durkheim, and reductionistic approaches in general, see Ninian Smart, *The Philosophy of Religion* (New York: Oxford University Press, 1979), chapter 6.

16. W. V. O. Quine, essay (untitled) in *What I Believe*, ed. Mark Booth (New York: Crossroad Publishing Company, 1984), 74; my emphasis.

17. Sigmund Freud, *Moses and Monotheism*, trans. Katherine Jones (London: Hogarth Press, 1951), 193–94.

18. Bertrand Russell, *Why I Am Not A Christian* (New York: George Allen and Unwin, 1957), 50–51.

Given Russell's attitudes about religion, he must have been disconcerted with James when, in 1919, he reported that he "was astonished" to find that Wittgenstein had "become a complete mystic," and that "[i]t all started from William James's *Varieties of Religious Experience*." (*Ludwig Wittgenstein, Letters To Russell, Keynes and Moore*, ed. with an Introduction by G. H. von Wright [Ithaca, N.Y.: Cornell University Press, 1974], 82). For Wittgenstein's own strongly positive response to *Varieties*, see Ray Monk, *Wittgenstein: The Duty of Genius* (New York: Macmillan Publishing Company, 1990), 51, 112. I am indebted to Robert Goff for calling my attention to these works.

19. Emphasis removed.
20. Among those who regard *Varieties* as just an empirical study, see A. J. Ayer, "Introduction" to *Pragmatism* and *The Meaning of Truth* (Cambridge: Harvard University Press, 1978), viii; Bennett Ramsey, *Submitting to Freedom: The Religious Vision of William James* (Oxford: Oxford University Press, 1993), 86; Russell B. Goodman, *American Philosophy and the Romantic Tradition* (Cambridge: Cambridge University Press, 1990), chapter 3. Others appreciate the philosophical nature of James's project. See especially James H. Leuba, "Professor William James' Interpretation of Religious Experience," *International Journal of Ethics* 14 (April, 1904): 323–24; Ralph Barton Perry, TC, 2:333–34; and Smith, "Introduction" to *Varieties,* xxxvi.
21. The initials "G. S. H." are those of Granville Stanley Hall, a psychologist who was a contemporary of James (EPH, 194). See also VRE, Lecture XVIII, especially 352; PU, 149; "Philosophical Conceptions and Practical Results," P, 264–66. See also the following claim by James:

> The logician's bias has always been too much with them. They have preferred the thinner to the thicker method, dialectical abstraction being so much more dignified and academic than the confused and unwholesome facts of personal biography. (PU, 139–40; see also 149)

It is interesting that in assisting Frank Abauzit in doing the French translation of *Varieties,* James was concerned that in Abauzit's desire for more extensive documentation of sources than James provided in the original, he was turning the book into a "work of erudition." "Whatever you make of my book," James sardonically cautioned, "you can't turn it into a scholarly work!" (VRE, 508–9). I suggest that James was concerned about this because he felt it would undermine the purpose of *Varieties* if it were perceived as just another academic project. James's intention in *Varieties* is to invite his readers to shed the usual academic accouterments and to participate, if only by proxy, in the wide range of experiences he presents.
22. See, for example, VRE, 351–52; P, 39–40, 260–62.

23. "It may be that possibility and permission . . . are all that the religious consciousness requires to live on" (VRE, 339).

2. The Challenge to Religion

1. Freud continues:

[B]y asking this question one is merely admitting to a store of unsatisfied libido to which something else must have happened, a kind of fermentation leading to sadness and depression. (Letter to Marie Bonaparte, August 13, 1937, in *Letters of Sigmund Freud,* ed. E. L. Freud, trans. James Stern and Tania Stern [New York: Basic Books, 1960], 436)

Freud's colleague Theodor Reik appears to have a similar philosophy of life. He makes the following judgment about the composer Gustav Mahler:

In his passionate desire to reach the ideal, this man neglected to live as other men. . . . He sought for the hidden metaphysical truth behind and beyond the phenomena of this world, for the ideals. He never tired in his search after that transcendental and supernatural secret of the Absolute and did not recognize that the great secret of the transcendental, the miracle of the metaphysical, is that it does not exist. (*The Haunting Melody* [New York: Farrar, Straus and Young, 1953], 344)

2. Albert Camus, "The Myth of Sisyphus," in *The Myth of Sisyphus and Other Essays,* trans. J. O'Brien (New York: Alfred A. Knopf, 1955).

3. R. M. Hare, "Nothing Matters," in *Applications of Moral Philosophy* (Berkeley: University of California Press, 1972), 33–34.

4. Thomas Nagel, "The Absurd," *Journal of Philosophy* 68, no. 20 (October 21, 1971).

5. Ibid., 718.

6. Ibid.

7. Ibid., 718–20.

8. Physicist Richard Feynman, for example, reports a feeling of "scientific awe" for the "mathematical beauty of nature." It is perhaps the lack of resiliency of his own concept of the religious which leads him to commit only to the description of this feeling as one which is "*analogous* to the feeling one has in religion." (*Surely You're Joking, Mr. Feynman!* [New York: Bantam Books, 1986], 237; my emphasis.)

Albert Einstein is more generous with what he will include under the category of the religious, while still being as cautious as Feynman about rejecting the idea of a personal God:

> The most beautiful thing we can experience is the mysterious. . . . To know that what is impenetrable to us really exists, manifesting itself as the highest wisdom and the most radiant beauty which our dull faculties can comprehend only in their most primitive forms—this knowledge, this feeling, is at the center of true religiousness. In this sense, and in this sense only, I belong in the ranks of devoutly religious men. (Albert Einstein et al., *Living Philosophies* [New York: Simon and Schuster, 1931], 6)

9. I qualify my remarks here to "most religious belief," since it may be argued that some forms of Buddhism may be excluded from this description.

10. See also VRE, 374–75; WB, 52–55. Also interesting in this regard is James's essay, "On a Certain Blindness in Human Beings," (particularly TT, 144), where he develops the notion of perceiving meaning in a world which we ordinarily take for granted. Note, also, that rather than following the more common opinion that if S loves Y he will find it more difficult to gain objective knowledge of Y (S's judgments will be biased in Y's favor), James believes that love puts S in a uniquely strong position to know Y. For a similar argument, see Robert Solomon, "The Virtue of Love," *Midwest Studies in Philosophy*, vol 13 (Notre Dame, Ind.: University of Notre Dame Press, 1988).

11. "The awe-inspiring and fascinating mystery." Rudolph Otto, *The Idea of the Holy* (Oxford: Oxford University Press, 1923).

12. William Blake, "Auguries of Innocence," in Arthur M. Eastman et al., eds., *The Norton Anthology of Poetry* (New York: W. W. Norton & Company, 1970), 533.

13. Gerard Manley Hopkins, "God's Grandeur," in *The Norton Anthology of Poetry*, 887.

14. Simone Weil, *Waiting for God* (New York: G. P. Putnam's Sons, 1951), 175.

15. Thomas Merton, *The Seven Storey Mountain* (New York: Harcourt Brace Jovanovich, 1948), 56.

The life of Gandhi also demonstrates the way in which religious meaning may transform the activities of daily life. Ved Mehta, for example, in his biography of Gandhi, reports that Gandhi had reverence for manual labor (*Mahatma Gandhi and His Apostles* [New York: Penguin Books, 1977], 19), and describes an incident in which Gandhi and his wife argued over who was going to clean the dirty linen of a madman who had tried to set Gandhi's wife on fire. Each wanted to do so. (Gandhi prevailed.) Mehta reports: "[Gandhi] never missed an opportunity to show us what an elevated and holy office it was to clean up someone else's excrement" (13). While this may seem extreme, its very extremity may help us to clarify the religious sensibility. When does devoutness shade into fanaticism?

16. As the copious literature in this field indicates, the concept of interpretation is a rich one, which itself may be variously interpreted. For a good overview regarding some of the central issues involved in this concept, see *The Interpretive Turn,* ed. David R. Hiley, James F. Bohman, and Richard Shusterman (Ithaca, N.Y.: Cornell University Press, 1991).

17. I do not mention nihilistic ethical positions, since on these views there is no objective ethical value for which a foundation could be sought.

18. See John Stuart Mill, *Utilitarianism,* ed. Samuel Gorovitz (New York: The Bobbs Merrill Company, 1971), chapter 2.

19. Bernard Williams, *Morality* (New York: Harper and Row, 1972), chapter 1.

20. In chapter 7, we shall more fully consider the role of interpretation in James's analysis of the meaning of religious

beliefs. As we shall see, his view is far more complicated than it may at first appear.

21. Ninian Smart makes the following claim about reductionism:

> [T]he danger of reductionism is to render the phenomenon being reduced unintelligible (like trying to reduce music to arrangements of sounds, without seeing that music has its own form of manifestation, beyond the sounds, so to say).
> (*The Philosophy of Religion*, 183)

22. These are the words used by Hugo Munsterberg to describe this pietà, in *The Crown of Life: Artistic Creativity in Old Age* (San Diego: Harcourt Brace Jovanovich, 1983), 17. In the following description, does poet Natalie Goldberg go too far in terms of what she thinks is a perceptible quality? What criteria would we need to decide this question, and what do those criteria presuppose?:

> If you read a lot of haiku, you see there is a leap that happens, a moment where the poet makes a large jump and the reader's mind must catch up. This creates a little sensation of space in the reader's mind, which is nothing less than a moment's experience of god. . . . (*Writing Down the Bones* [Boston: Shambhala Publications, 1986], 125)

23. Indeed, no observable properties are ever really simple, for James. He holds that beyond the "blooming, buzzing confusion" (PP, 1:462), everything we perceive is conditioned by our values, purposes, and interests. For further discussion of this point, see PPWJ, chapter 2. For more recent neurobiological support of a view such as James's, see, for example, Semir Zeki, "The Visual Image in Mind and Brain," *Scientific American* 267, no. 3 (September, 1992). Zeki reports on brain research which indicates that "the integration of visual information is a process in which perception and comprehension of the visual world occur simultaneously" (76). I am indebted to Michael Seid for calling my attention to this article.

24. Consider what it would be like if the people we call art and music critics were unable to discern the deeper meanings of the objects of their analysis.

25. In "The Will to Believe" James makes the following claim about the relationship between religious belief and moral service.

> This feeling . . . that by obstinately believing that there are gods . . . we are doing the universe the deepest service we can, seems part of the living essence of the religious hypothesis. (WB, 31)

See also the following claim in *Varieties:*

> We and God have business with each other; and in opening ourselves to his influence our deepest destiny is fulfilled. The universe, at those parts of it which our personal being constitutes, takes a turn genuinely for the worse or for the better in proportion as each one of us fulfills or evades God's demands. (VRE, 406–7)

For a fuller discussion of James's view of our religious responsibilities, see chapter 6.

26. Acts 9: 1–22. I refer to St. Paul to indicate the context of his religious decision, rather than its content. St. Paul's decision, of course, was not whether to believe in God at all, but whether to convert from Judaism to Christianity.

27. Compare both Aristotle (*Nichomachean Ethics,* 1100 a 4 ff.; 1101 a 14–20) and Mill (*Utilitarianism,* 21–22) on the related notion that the determination of whether someone is happy can only be made by judging the person's life as a whole.

28. James's theories of meaning and truth are prime examples of this. See PPWJ, chapters 3 and 6, for further discussion.

29. I omit more sectarian claims regarding the beneficial consequences of religious belief. It may be claimed that if God exists, believers will be immortal, and receive the eternal rewards in heaven which are available only to the faithful, etc. Perhaps it is with these sorts of consequences in mind that we should understand James's ill-advised, more flagrantly utilitarian claim that religious belief offers us our "sole chance in life of getting upon the winning side" (WB, 31).

30. It is interesting that imagination also has an important role in ethical arguments. For without appeal to moral imagi-

nation, it is questionable whether one could even begin to
make arguments against ethical scepticism or moral fanaticism.
See R. M. Hare, *Freedom and Reason* (New York: Oxford University Press, 1963), chapter 9.

31. See also the following claim by James:

> I . . . for one, cannot see my way to accepting the agnostic
> rules for truth-seeking. . . . I cannot do so for this plain
> reason, that a rule of thinking which would absolutely prevent me from acknowledging certain kinds of truth if those
> kinds of truth were really there, would be an irrational rule.
> (WB, 31–32)

3. PRECONCEPTUAL KNOWLEDGE

1. See also VRE, 358–60.
2. See also VRE, 405, WB, 77. The following passage provides another striking expression of James's position:

> If you have intuitions at all, they come from a deeper level
> of your nature than the loquacious level which rationalism
> inhabits. Your whole subconscious life, your impulses, your
> faiths, your needs, your divinations, have prepared the
> premises, of which your consciousness now feels the weight
> of the result; and something in you absolutely *knows* that
> the result must be truer than any logic-chopping rationalistic talk, however clever, that may contradict it. (VRE, 67)

Note also William Clebsch's remark:

> For James . . . propositional proofs [of God's existence]
> made so serious-minded an option trivial; propositional
> refutations made it fatuous. (*American Religious Thought: A
> History* [Chicago: University of Chicago Press, 1973], 162)

3. See also the following:

> Music gives us ontological messages which non-musical
> criticism is unable to contradict, though it may laugh at our
> foolishness in minding them. (VRE, 334; see also 304)

4. It is interesting to observe that while James appeals to
the idea of music as a form of direct knowledge to help develop his ideas in the philosophy of religion, his philosophy
in turn has been cited by the composer Aaron Copeland in the
attempt to explain musical meaning. Copeland finds James
helpful as he analyzes what he takes to be the limitations of
Paul Hindemith's theories of music:

> The Hindemithian theories will always have most appeal to
> those minds that feel comfortable only with a closely rea-
> soned and systematic approach to any problem. My own
> mind feels more at home with the unsystematic approach of
> writers like Montaigne and Goethe, let us say; and especially
> in the field of music it seems to me important that we keep
> open what William James calls the "irrational doorways . . .
> through which . . . the wildness and the pang of life" may be
> glimpsed. The systematic and the irrational are mutually ex-
> clusive; and that is why Hindemith's tenets, clarified and
> truthful as far as they go, are inherently limited and cannot
> hope to encompass the oftentimes instinctual drives of the
> creative mechanism. (*Music and Imagination* [Cambridge:
> Harvard University Press, 1952], 66)

Hindemith, however, asks questions which shift the ground
of this debate and raise an important philosophical and artistic
issue:

> Although the creative process in its highest stages may always
> remain hidden from human comprehension, as may the mys-
> terious source of artistic work in general, yet the dividing
> point between conscious and unconscious work can be raised
> to an extraordinary degree. If this were not true, everyone in
> whom this point lies at a very low level could assert that he is
> creating the greatest works of art. There would be no differ-
> ence between Beethoven and any other composer, who had
> with difficulty achieved a mere quarter, say, of the height of
> artistic achievement that men may attain, and knew nothing
> of the other three quarters that still lay above him. Such a
> little man would not care to speak of technical matters, but

would instead refer to his impulse, his feeling, his heart, which had prescribed the way for him. But must not this impulse be tiny and this feeling negligible if they can express themselves with so little knowledge? Is not an immense mastery of the medium needed to translate into tones what the heart dictates? (*The Craft of Musical Composition, Book 1, Theoretical Part*, 4th ed., trans. Arthur Mendel [London: Schott & Co., 1942], 11–12)

5. Abraham Joshua Heschel, *The Insecurity of Freedom* (New York: Schocken Books, 1972), 245.

Note also similar claims by contemporaries of James, for example Ernest Renan, a thinker of whom James often disapproved, but nevertheless sometimes quoted from memory (TC, 2:285). Renan holds that music and opera are capable of extending thought into realms inexpressible in words:

La philosophie moderne aura de même sa dernière expression dans un drame, ou plutôt dans un opéra; car la musique et les illusions de la scène lyrique serviraient admirablement à continuer la pensée, au moment où la parole ne suffit plus à l'exprimer. (Preface to *Drames Philosophiques* [Paris: Calmann-Levy, 1888])

See also the following claim by a German near-contemporary of James, musicologist Gustav Schilling. I suggest we read Schilling in this passage not as suggesting that art actually transcends the sphere of cognition, but rather that it transcends the domain of conceptual knowledge:

Romantic art springs from man's attempt to transcend the sphere of cognition, to experience higher, more spiritual things, and to sense the presence of the ineffable. No aesthetic material is better suited to the expression of the ineffable than is sound, the stuff of music. . . . Music on the wings of rhythm can achieve that which no color, however splendid, no chisel, no word can achieve. The proper realm of true music only begins where speech leaves off. (Translated from *Enclyclopädie der gesammten musikalischen Wissenschaften, oder Universal Lexikon der Tonkunst* (1834–38), in

Peter le Huray and James Day, eds., *Music and Aesthetics in the Eighteenth and Early-Nineteenth Centuries* [Cambridge: Cambridge University Press, 1981], 470)

Finally, consider these frequently quoted remarks by Felix Mendelssohn:

> People usually complain that music is so ambiguous; that it is so doubtful what they ought to think when they hear it; whereas everyone understands words. With me it is entirely the converse. And not only with regard to an entire speech, but also with individual words; these, too, seem to me to be so ambiguous, so vague, and so easily misunderstood in comparison with genuine music, which fills the soul with a thousand things better than words. The thoughts which are expressed to me by a piece of music which I love are not too indefinite to be put into words, but on the contrary too definite. (Letter to Marc André Souchay, October 5, 1842, cited in Deryck Cooke, *The Language of Music* [Oxford: Oxford University Press, 1959], 12)

6. Note, for example, the way in which Hasidic Jews reject the intellect in favor of mystical, intuitional, and emotional modalities. Rabbi Israel Baal Shem Tov, the founder of modern Hasidism, rejected the intellectual sphere as strongly as the scientific rationalist rejects the religious. Elie Wiesel describes and supports the Baal Shem's position as such:

> The Baal Shem's call was a call to subjectivity, to passionate involvement; the tales he told and those told about him appeal to the imagination rather than reason. They try to prove that man is more than he appears to be and that he is capable of giving more than he appears to possess. To dissect them, therefore, is to diminish them. To judge them is to detach oneself and taint their candor—in so doing, one loses more than one could gain. (*Souls on Fire: Portraits and Legends of Hasidic Masters* [New York: Summit Books, 1972], 7)

7. PP, 1:217. The origination of this distinction is often misattributed to Bertrand Russell. In fact, it is not original

with James either. After introducing the distinction, James adds a note referring his readers to Grote and Helmholtz.

8. See also Carolyn Heilbrun's suggestion, in her book on biography, that a biographer who is the same nationality, religion, or gender of his or her subject is, ceterus paribus, more likely to render a more penetrating and accurate interpretation of that subject's life. (*Writing a Woman's Life* [New York: Ballantine Books, 1988], 50–53).

9. Dance notator Sandra Aberkains provides another example of knowledge that is not propositional. She discusses how in some instances the experience of dance cannot be represented by symbols, in this case, dance notation:

> The sections of dances that are difficult to notate are also the ones that are difficult for the dancers to learn or for new dancers to absorb. They usually don't depend on things you can talk about easily, and their movement is sometimes not even really set. Their performance often has to do with the feel of the group. ("Dance," in *New Yorker*, 30 July 1990, 5)

It is interesting that while Aberkains suggests that insights may transcend language, author John Updike considers how language itself may take us beyond literal apprehension. Indeed, it is capable of doing so in ways a visual medium may not be. In observing that Kafka's description of the insect in "The Metamorphosis" is deliberately vague, Updike underscores the great potential of the verbal medium, by which Kafka is able to fulfill his literary intentions:

> Such scenes could not be done except with words. In this age that lives and dies by the visual, "The Metamorphosis" stands as a narrative absolutely literary, able to exist only where language and the mind's hazy wealth of imagery intersect. (Forward to Franz Kafka, *The Complete Stories* [New York: Schocken Books, 1971], xvi)

Of course in the case of visual art it would be foolish to expect verbal equivalents. Language as a social construct can achieve only so much. The following is from a discussion of Michelangelo's Florence pietà, of the early 1550s:

[The meanings in] Michelangelo's group . . . are probably never wholly accessible to verbal definition, distilled and recombined as they are by his unequaled powers of emotional and plastic expression. (David Finn, text by Frederick Hartt, *Michelangelo's Three Pietàs: A Photographic Study* [New York: Harry N. Abrams, 1975], 88)

10. Letter to Jacques Hadamard, in Brewster Ghiselin, *The Creative Process* (Berkeley: University of California Press, 1952), 43–44. See a similar view in Evelyn Fox Keller's biography of geneticist Barbara McClintock, *A Feeling for the Organism* (New York: W. H. Freeman and Company, 1983), especially 143–51, 197–207.

11. See, for example, Arthur Koestler, *The Act of Creation* (London: Arkana Press, 1989), 118. It was also in a dream that the Russian scientist Dmitri Ivanovitch Mendeleev is said to have discovered the form of the periodic table of the chemical elements. See P. W. Atkins, *The Periodic Kingdom* (New York: Basic Books, 1995), 83–87.

12. For a full and stimulating analysis of the way in which scientific imagination functions, see Gerald Holton, *The Scientific Imagination: Case Studies* (Cambridge: Cambridge University Press, 1978). Also interesting in this regard is the following passage in a letter Ernst Mach wrote to James after he read *Varieties:*

Your fine and remarkable book, *The Varieties of Religious Experience,* has gripped me powerfully. Religious inspiration is certainly very similar to the scientific inspiration which one feels when new problems first present themselves in a form which is as yet not wholly clear. There is an as yet unmeasured depth into which one is gazing. (TC, 2:341)

Goodman, in *American Philosophy and the Romantic Tradition,* 70, cites an interesting description of James by his student Dickinson S. Miller (originally published in LWJ, 2:12–13). It provides a biographical context for James's support of intuitive knowledge. Miller reports:

[James] was really not argumentative, not inclined to dialectic or pertinacious debate of any sort. It must always have required an effort of self-control to put up with it. He almost never, even in private conversation, contended for his own opinion. He had a way of often falling back on the language of perception, insight, sensibility, vision of possibilities.

13. See, for example, Hans Reichenbach, *Experience and Prediction* (Chicago: University of Chicago Press, 1938), chapter 1, section 1, for his discussion in support of a strict distinction between the contexts of discovery and justification.

14. See, for example, Keller, *A Feeling for the Organism,* and Paul Feyerabend, *Against Method,* rev. ed. (London: Verso, 1988), who both contend that the actual practice of science does not reflect the philosophers' of science idealized models of it.

15. Mark Johnson, *The Body in the Mind* (Chicago: University of Chicago Press, 1987). See also George Lakoff and Mark Johnson, *Metaphors We Live By* (Chicago: University of Chicago Press, 1980).

16. Johnson, *The Body in the Mind,* xiv.

17. Ibid., 13.

18. Ibid., 175.

19. Ibid., 220, n. 18.

20. Ibid., 175.

21. See PPWJ, chapters 2, 3, 6, and 7; and especially chapter 8 of Johnson, *The Body in the Mind.*

22. Richard Viladesau, "Music as an Approach to God," *Catholic World* 232, no. 1387, January / February, 1989, 5.

23. Ibid., 7.

24. Ibid., 4–5.

25. Ibid., 5. What might be the mechanism by which such reflection is explained? While Viladesau does not elaborate, one possible explanation might be that we are able both to express and discern the divine through music because God has created us with an innate capacity to do so. Consider C.S. Lewis's similar claim in *Mere Christianity* (New York: Macmillan Publishing Company, 1943), 26–35, that moral feelings are universal because they are imprinted on us by God.

26. John Hospers, *Meaning and Truth in the Arts* (Chapel Hill: University of North Carolina Press, 1946), 227–38.

27. Hospers is one of those who incorrectly attributes the origination of this distinction to Bertrand Russell. See *Meaning and Truth in the Arts,* 233.

28. Ibid., 235.

29. D. W. Gotshalk, *Art and the Social Order* (Chicago: University of Chicago Press, 1947).

30. Ibid., 149–51. For further discussion of Gotshalk see also John Passmore, *Serious Art* (London: Duckworth, 1991), 115–17.

31. Arthur Schopenhauer, *The World as Will and Idea* (London: Routledge and Kegan Paul, 1957), 1:336.

32. Beethoven's friend Bettina von Arnim quotes him as saying that "I must despise the world which does not know that music is a higher revelation than all wisdom and philosophy." (O. G. Sonneck, ed., *Beethoven: Impressions by his Contemporaries* [New York: Dover Publications, 1967], 80). See also J. W. N. Sullivan, *Beethoven: His Spiritual Development* (New York: Vintage Books, 1960).

For another composer's view, consider the following by Ralph Vaughan Williams in the opening lines of his essay "What is Music?":

> [M]usic is a reaching out to the ultimate realities by means of ordered sound. . . . But it may be asked what does music mean? A lot of nonsense is talked nowadays about the 'meaning' of music. Music indeed has a meaning, though it is not one that can be expressed in words. Mendelssohn used to say that the meaning of music was too precise for words. . . . [I]t is these great patterns in sound, designed by Beethoven or Bach, which open the magic casements and enable us to understand what is beyond the appearances of life. (*National Music and Other Essays* [Oxford: Oxford University Press, 1987], 206)

33. Among the other philosophers who have noticed this problem are J. L. Mackie, *The Miracle of Theism* (Oxford: Oxford University Press, 1982), 182; and Peter Jones, "William

James," in M. G. Singer, ed., *American Philosophy* (Cambridge: Cambridge University Press, 1985), 56–57.

34. Of course, this is not to make the sceptical challenges disappear by a mere semantic device. For if the direct experience of God in cases of "revelation" makes it impossible for the sceptic meaningfully to ask "Is this revelation reliable?" the sceptic need only ask, "Is this experience one of genuine revelation?"

35. For James's use of the term "revelation" in the context of his discussion of mystical experience, see VRE, 324. In James's estimation, an experience belongs on the continuum of revelatory experiences if it has an effect, however small, in opening up the subject to a deeper and more significant dimension of reality, inacessible by ordinary mental states. James includes drug and alcohol experiences as points along this continuum, as ways (albeit ones which are seriously flawed) of approaching a more meaningful level of reality (VRE, 307–8).

Given James's position, Betrand Russell's quip about mystical states is particularly relevant:

> In our own day, as William James has related [in *Varieties*], there have been people who considered that the intoxication produced by laughing gas revealed truths which are hidden at normal times. From a scientific point of view, we can make no distinction between a man who eats little and sees heaven and a man who drinks much and sees snakes. Each is in an abnormal physical condition, and therefore has abnormal perceptions. (*Religion and Science* [Oxford: Oxford University Press, 1961], 188)

There is no reason, however, to think that Russell has had the last word. In Lecture I of *Varieties,* James argues robustly against the view, held by Russell and others, that "abnormal" (in the sense of unusual) physical conditions necessarily engender "abnormal" (in the sense of distorted or unreliable) perceptions.

36. He also offers two other characteristics—transiency and passivity—which he regards as typical of mystical states, but as neither necessary nor sufficient conditions of them.

37. Merton, *The Seven Storey Mountain*, 284–85. See also the long quotation James gives from St. John of the Cross, VRE, 323.

38. George Nakhnikian, "On the Cognitive Import of Certain Conscious States," in Sidney Hook, ed., *Religious Experience and Truth* (New York: New York University Press, 1961), 163.

39. TC, 2:350. This remark was made in response to criticism by James H. Leuba. For more on Leuba's critique and James's response, see TC, 2:347–51.

For a related comment, see James's June 16, 1901 letter to Henry W. Rankin:

> The impressions and impulsions and emotions and excitements which we . . . receive [through our religious consciousness] help us to live, they found invincible assurance of a world beyond the sense, they melt our hearts and commmunicate significance and value to everything and make us happy. (LWJ, 2:150)

40. Daya Krishna, "Religious Experience, Language, and Truth," in Sidney Hook, ed., *Religious Experience and Truth*, 239.

41. TC, 2:331.

4. The Cognitive Value of Feelings

1. Indeed, nineteenth-century Protestant theologian Friedrich Schleiermacher has argued that the profound feelings engendered by the religious life are its ultimate justification. See especially his *Soliloquies*, trans. Horace Leland Friess (Chicago: Open Court Publishing Company, 1957). Given his remarks in "The Dilemma of Determinism" (WB, 128–31), I suspect that James would reject Schleiermacher's view as morally intolerable sentimentalism.

2. James's view that feelings may be cognitive might seem odd in light of his analysis, in *The Principles of Psychology*, of emotions as reducible to physiological states. For a good explanation of how James's understanding, in *Varieties*, of the role

of the religious emotion, is not inconsistent with his theory of emotion in *The Principles,* see Gerald E. Myers, *William James* (New Haven: Yale University Press, 1986), 466–68. See also 461, 478–80, for additional discussion on James's view of religious emotions.

A number of philosophers in addition to Myers have acknowledged the cognitive role of feelings in James's philosophy, holding positions quite different from my own. See, for example, William Joseph Gavin, *William James and the Reinstatement of the Vague* (Philadelphia: Temple University Press, 1992), Part I; Eugene Fontinell, *Self, God and Immortality* (Philadelphia: Temple University Press, 1986), 13, 62–64; Levinson, *The Religious Investigations of William James,* 172–89; Goodman, *American Philosophy and the Romantic Tradition,* 22–23, 32–33, 70–80; and Charlene Haddock Seigfried, *William James's Radical Reconstruction of Philosophy* (Albany: State University of New York Press, 1990), 125.

For a related discussion of feelings, see John J. McDermott, "Feeling as Insight: The Affective Dimension of Social Diagnosis," in *The Culture of Experience: Philosophical Essays in the American Grain* (New York: New York University Press, 1976).

3. Nakhnikian joins the commentators on James in not distinguishing between feelings and emotions in the discussion of this issue. In the current context, neither I, James, nor the other philosophers I will be discussing differentiate between "emotions" and "feelings"—the terms are used interchangeably. For our purposes, then, "feeling" is not to be understood narrowly as referring only to bodily sensations (such as a feeling of pain), but more broadly to incorporate phenomena such as feelings of wonder, awe, etc.

4. Nakhnikian, "On the Cognitive Import of Certain Conscious States," in Sidney Hook, ed., *Religious Experience and Truth,* 160.

5. Ibid., 161–62.

6. Ibid., 162.

7. A circle is the most simple example of a plane curve. For a thorough discussion of Kepler's process of discovery, see

Alexandre Koyré, *The Astronomical Revolution* (New York: Dover Books, 1992).

8. Carl Hempel, *Philosophy of Natural Science* (Englewood Cliffs, N.J.: Prentice Hall, 1966), 40–45.

9. Gilbert Harman, "Inference to the Best Explanation," *Philosophical Review* 74, no. 1 (January, 1965), 88–95.

10. Peter Lipton, *Inference to the Best Explanation* (London: Routledge, 1991), 119.

11. Ibid. See especially chapters 4 and 7.

12. This idea, to which James would fully agree, is developed from a point made by Lipton, *Inference to the Best Explanation*, 124.

13. As Aristotle enjoined, "[I]t is the mark of an educated man to look for precision in each class of things just so far as the subject admits" (*Nichomachean Ethics*, 1094 b 25).

14. See, for example, James's lecture notes to his Philosophy of Nature course of 1902–3. In considering putative objections to the position that minds are conterminous, James cites an objection to the view and his reply to it: "'Preestablished harmony is a better theory.' Answer: No, for it violates parsimony" (ML, 269).

15. For a related view by a contemporary philosopher of science, see Mary Hesse, who claims that science is largely devoid of the richer elements of human meaning, and for this reason cannot compete with traditional religions. "Physics, Philosophy, and Myth," in Robert J. Russell, William R. Stoeger, S.J., and George V. Coyne, S.J., eds., *Physics, Philosophy and Theology: A Common Quest for Understanding* (Vatican City State: Vatican Observatory, 1988), 198–99.

16. Myers, *William James*, 461; see also 478.

17. Ibid.

18. Nor does James believe, as Myers suggests (478), that the universe will fulfill our deepest yearnings. James has a healthy respect for the problem of evil. See, for example, his lectures on "The Sick Soul" in *Varieties* (especially 136–38), as well as his discussions of evil in "The Dilemma of Determinism" (especially WB, 125–37) and "Is Life Worth Living?" in WB.

19. James makes the same point again, in somewhat different terms:

> [A] philosophy which utterly denies all fundamental ground for seriousness, for effort, for hope, which says the nature of things is radically alien to human nature, can never succeed. . . . (WB, 75)

Points such as these appear throughout "The Sentiment of Rationality" and "Reflex Action and Theism," in WB.

20. It is only the beginning point, however. In "The Will to Believe" and elsewhere, James is careful to protect himself against a philosophy of wishful thinking. See PPWJ, chapter 5.

21. Note Goodman's observation (*American Philosophy and The Romantic Tradition,* 22–23), of the much stronger suggestion explored by Stanley Cavell, that certain feelings are not just natural, but *inescapable,* and that because they are inescapable, they are revelatory. Goodman cites Cavell's *Must we Mean What We Say?* (Cambridge: Cambridge University Press, 1969), 324 n. 15, and *The Senses of Walden: An Expanded Edition* (San Francisco: North Point Press, 1981), 104.

22. Oliver Sacks, "An Anthropologist on Mars," in *An Anthropologist on Mars: Seven Paradoxical Tales* (New York: Alfred A. Knopf, 1995).

23. Ibid., 293.

24. Ibid., 287–88.

25. For a related argument, see WB, 51. Of course it is no small point against the parallel I have drawn between ordinary empirical and religious knowledge that we have an established scientific theory to explain the normal observer's perceptions of physical objects, while we do not have such a theory in religion. But the point, of course, is that it makes no sense to ask for a scientific theory in the context of religion. I do not think that the lack of such a theory obviates the parallels I am drawing here. The fact that we do not yet have a way to explain the relationship between religious feelings and what they purport to indicate is not enough to deny the possibility of their cognitive import.

26. Of course, as I have suggested above, what counts as evidence is itself determined in part pragmatically.

5. Truth in Religion

1. PPWJ, chapter 6.

2. I shall retain James's meaning, and use the term "verifiable" as interchangeable with "confirmable," or "progressively confirmable by experience." While in some contexts this use of language might cause difficulties, it should not do so in the current discussion.

3. I have argued extensively in PPWJ, chapter 6, and so will not repeat my arguments here, that for James the notion of a belief being satisfactory is considerably different from its simply being subjectively satisfying.

4. It is interesting that later, in *The Meaning of Truth*, 5, in what seems to be pique at his adversaries' lack of intellectual charity, James rescinds this claim. But as far as I can tell, he does so only for rhetorical purposes and not because there is a genuine change in his position.

5. Bertrand Russell, "William James's Conception of Truth," *Philosophical Essays* (New York: Simon and Schuster, 1968), 125. Russell's article was originally published as "Transatlantic 'Truth'," *Albany Review*, January 1908.

6. A. J. Ayer, *The Origins of Pragmatism* (San Francisco: Freeman, Cooper and Company, 1968), 213.

7. Ibid.

8. Ibid., 212.

9. See, for example, C. S. Peirce, "The most that can be maintained is, that we seek for a belief that we shall *think* to be true. But we think each one of our beliefs to be true, and, indeed, it is mere tautology to say so." ("The Fixation of Belief," in Charles Hartshorne and Paul Weiss, eds., *Collected Papers of Charles Sanders Peirce* [Cambridge: Harvard University Press, 1934], 5.375. Citation is to volume and section number.)

10. See especially *Pragmatism*, 96, 112. See also "Remarks on Spencer," EPH, especially 18–22; MT, 50–51. For a full discussion of James's conception of the active, interested, and purposive nature of cognition, see PPWJ, chapter 2.

11. See also PP, 2:1179; WB, 78.

12. See also WB, 66; EPS, 271; PP, 2:1260. See also similar remarks of John Paul II, "Message of His Holiness Pope

John Paul II," in Russell, Stoeger, S.J., and Coyne, S.J., *Physics, Philosophy and Theology*, M8–M9.

13. Thomas Kuhn, *The Structure of Scientific Revolutions*, 2d ed. (Chicago: University of Chicago Press, 1970).

14. The preceding discussion has been my own analysis of how, given the principles of James's philosophy, he is able to respond successfully to Russell's critique. James offers his own response to Russell in "Two English Critics" in *The Meaning of Truth*. His reply is rather vague and half-hearted, however, all the more disappointing given what it might have been. I explain James's lackluster response in part by his distaste for adversarial acrobatics in philosophy. See Dickinson Miller's remark above, in note 12 of chapter 3.

15. Hilary Putnam, *Reason, Truth and History* (Cambridge: Cambridge University Press, 1981), and *The Many Faces of Realism* (La Salle, Ill.: Open Court Publishing Company, 1987). Not wanting to complicate matters in ways which are distracting from the main point of this discussion, I shall omit consideration of how James is importantly different from the current neopragmatists. In fact, along with his own version of "internal realism" James also (albeit not consistently) accepts some aspects of metaphysical realism as well. For a full discussion of this issue, see PPWJ, chapter 6, especially 105–15. Finally, it might be interesting to compare Putnam's "internal realism" to the various versions of "critical realism" proposed earlier in the twentieth century.

16. In *The Language of Morals* (New York: Oxford University Press, 1964), chapter 6, R. M. Hare makes a similar point about the term "good." He sees "good" as a general term of approbation, whose specific criteria of application can only be specified by reference to the context in which it is used. James's comment in *Pragmatism*, 42, that "truth is *one species of good*" is particularly interesting in this regard.

17. The idea that our efforts to explain and predict are based on what might be called a religious desire to find our place in the universe, is one which is worth pondering. If it were true, the enterprise of science would, broadly speaking, be in the service of religion. Indeed, in ancient times, the ful-

fillment of religious desires was a central motivating principle in sciences such as astronomy. See Anthony Aveni, *Conversing with the Planets: How Science and Myth Invented the Cosmos* (New York: Times Books, 1992).

18. See VRE, 392.

19. Ian Barbour, "Paradigms in Science and Religion," in Gary Gutting, ed., *Paradigms and Revolutions* (Notre Dame, Ind.: University of Notre Dame Press, 1980), 239.

20. Although both Smith ("Introduction" to VRE, xlvii), and Myers (*William James*, 466, 473), note that in *Varieties* James abandons his pragmatic approach to truth, neither offers an explanation as to why. I shall argue that James merely appears to abandon his pragmatic criterion of truth, but does not actually do so.

21. Later, in *Varieties*, and in *A Pluralistic Universe* (especially Lecture VIII), James renounces theism.

22. George Santayana, "William James," in *Character and Opinion in the United States* (New York: Charles Scribner's Sons, 1920), 67.

23. Ralph Barton Perry, *In the Spirit of William James* (Bloomington: Indiana University Press, 1958), 206–7.

24. Ralph Waldo Emerson, *Essays* (First Series) (Boston: Houghton, Mifflin and Company, 1904), 57.

25. Cotkin, *William James, Public Philosopher*. See especially 76–84. Of course, James also had his own more strictly philosophical reasons for developing his pragmatic methodology, which Cotkin does not discuss.

26. See, for example, the "Preface" to *The Will to Believe*, 7–8, where James is explicit about this strategy.

27. See especially "The Will to Believe" and "The Dilemma of Determinism," in WB.

28. In chapter 2, we have seen more fully the specific conditions under which James thinks belief on pragmatic grounds is justified.

29. There is reason to think, however, that James's position in *Varieties* contradicts whatever suggestion he may have made in *The Principles*, that the hypothesis of God's existence may be counted as a "postulate of rationality," which is in principle

unverifiable. See the discussion of the postulates of rationality earlier in this chapter.

30. See PPWJ, chapter 6. For a provocative article arguing that the concept of scientific verification is itself pragmatically interpreted in terms of satisfactory consequences, see More-land Perkins, "Notes on the Pragmatic Theory of Truth," *The Journal of Philosophy* 49, no. 18 (August 28, 1952).

31. PPWJ, chapter 5. See also chapter 2, above.

6. THE MORAL SIGNIFICANCE OF RELIGIOUS BELIEF

1. See TC, 2:583, where James laments the professional difficulties caused by his "free and easy style" in *Pragmatism*.

2. These admonitions are from the anonymous nineteenth-century Russian spiritual classic, *The Way of A Pilgrim*, published with *The Pilgrim Continues His Way*, trans. R. M. French (San Francisco: Harper San Francisco, 1973), 12, 22.

3. These are the words of twentieth-century Buddhist monk, Dainin Katagiri, *Returning to Silence* (Boston: Shambhala Publications, 1988), 15.

4. Thomas Merton, *The Sign of Jonas* (New York: Harcourt Brace Jovanovich, 1953), 120.

5. James defines the saintly character as "the character for which spiritual emotions are the habitual centre of the personal energy" (VRE, 219).

6. See also VRE, 328, where James explains why saints are often practically inept. Also interesting in this regard is the discussion in *The Principles of Psychology,* where James again highlights the normative element of religious belief. Here James suggests that one reason we posit God's existence is so that we may have an ideal judge to which we may appeal, one who would acknowledge and commend our morally best qualities, even if in fact they were to remain forever unacknowledged by our peers or future generations (PP, 2:301–2).

7. I owe this concept to Joseph Suckiel.

8. VRE, 283.

9. See, for example, PU, 142–43. In addition, in support of the many extreme forms of religion which James uses to develop his case, he argues that extreme cases may yield profounder truths (VRE, 303, 383; LWJ, 2:209); that it is easier to arrive at conclusions by using them (VRE, 48). Thus, one must be careful in deciding which pathologies to reject as genuinely distortive. This justification notwithstanding, it is interesting to note that soon after it appeared, according to Julius Bixler, *Varieties* was nicknamed "Wild Religions I have Known" (*Religion in the Philosophy of William James* [Boston: Marshall Jones Company, 1926], 1).

There are, of course, also disorders of institutionalized religion, which James suggests are not eliminable. James is outspoken in condemning the churches for "[stifling] the spontaneous religious spirit" (VRE, 270). He includes "hypocrisy and tyranny and meanness and tenacity of superstition" among the intrinsic flaws of institutionalized religions (VRE, 269).

10. See chapter 2, above, as well as PPWJ, chapter 5, for a fuller discussion of "The Will to Believe."

11. See J.L. Austin, "Performative-Constative," trans. G.J. Warnock, in Charles E. Caton, ed., *Philosophy and Ordinary Language* (Urbana: University of Illinois Press, 1963). It is also interesting to compare the "logic of commitment" in the faith ladder to the logic of James's avowal in a diary entry of April 30, 1870, that his "first act of free will shall be to believe in free will" (LWJ, 1:147).

12. He amplifies his point as follows:

"Will you or won't you have it so?" is the most probing question we are ever asked; we are asked it every hour of the day, and about the largest as well as the smallest, the most theoretical as well as the most practical, things. We answer by consents or non-consents and not by words. (PP, 2:1182)

13. One label given to "The Will to Believe," by James's critics. See Dickinson Miller, "'The Will to Believe' and the Duty to Doubt," *International Journal of Ethics* 9 (1898–99); P, 124; TC, 2:241.

14. Of course, given his conceptions of truth and reality, James's notion of reality "independent" of the subject is more complex than that of non-pragmatic, realist philosophers. See chapter 5 above, and PPWJ, chapters 6 and 7.

15. James asserts that the idea of an omniscient and omnipotent God is "a disease of the philosophy shop" (LWJ, 2:269). See also PU, 141.

16. See P, 136–38, 144.

17. SPP, 116–17, 229–30. See also VRE, 406–8; P, Lecture VIII; WB, 31.

18. See also VRE, 41–46, 406, 408; WB, 31, 160. While in "Reflex Action and Theism," James makes this claim in the course of developing an argument for theism, he maintains the notion of God's purposes even in his non-theistic writings. See PU, Lectures I and VIII. See also James's claim that both the divine and human personalities "have purposes for which they care, and each can hear the other's call" (WB, 98).

19. See also PU, 19, where James supports "the pantheistic field of vision, the vision of God as the indwelling divine rather than the external creator, and of human life as part and parcel of that deep reality."

20. James makes the following claim in *Some Problems of Philosophy:*

> [Faith] may be regarded as a formative factor in the universe, if we be integral parts thereof, and co-determinants, by our behavior, of what its total character may be. (SPP, 113. See also 111–12)

See also "The Sentiment of Rationality" (WB, 80–89), where James enters into a long discussion of how we may contribute to the moral nature of the world. Note also the following comment:

> Any mode of conceiving the universe which makes an appeal to [the power to trust], and makes the man seem as if he were individually helping to create the actuality of the truth whose metaphysical reality he is willing to assume, will be sure to be responded to by large numbers (WB, 76)

21. See also ERE, 89, as well as the following passage from *Varieties:*

> If religion be a function by which either God's cause or man's cause is to be really advanced, then he who lives the life of it, however narrowly, is a better servant than he who merely knows about it, however much. (VRE, 386)

22. See, for example, VRE, 405 ff.

23. Even though his incipient religious view slips through. See WB, 147–48, 159–62.

24. Assuming, of course, that they do not impede the possibility of the inclusive satisfaction of other demands. I discuss this more fully in PPWJ, chapter 4. See also TC, 2:265.

25. Note that God in "The Moral Philosopher" is conceived of as infinite, not finite, as James thinks of Him in *Varieties* and *A Pluralistic Universe.*

26. James equivocates on whether God *discerns* the most inclusive moral arrangement, or whether He *creates* it by virtue of His own desires. The following passage can be read either way:

> It would seem . . . that the stable and systematic moral universe for which the ethical philosopher asks is fully possible only in a world where there is a divine thinker with all-enveloping demands. If such a thinker existed, his way of subordinating the demands to one another would be the finally valid casuistic scale; his claims would be the most appealing; his ideal universe would be the most inclusive realizable whole. If he now exist, then actualized in his thought already must be that ethical philosophy which we seek as the pattern which our own must evermore approach. (WB, 161)

27. See TT, 243.

28. See TT, 182.

29. See also James's letter to his wife, July 29, 1896 (LWJ, 2:43).

30. See VRE, 210–34, passim.

31. I also discuss its deficiencies, in PPWJ, chapter 4.

32. James's avowed disdain for Kant notwithstanding. There are, of course, also profound differences between James's and Kant's ethical views.

33. For an illuminating discussion of James's conception of the philosophical text as a "spur," which points beyond itself, see Gavin, *William James and the Reinstatement of the Vague,* 186–93.

34. When James was giving the Edinburgh lectures which were later to be published as *Varieties,* he wrote to his friends to keep them apprised of his progress. In a postcard he sent to Josiah Royce on May 17, 1901, describing the occasion of his first lecture, James wrote:

> Well! I made the plunge yesterday. . . . I feel all right, and doubt not, Heaven helping its champion, that I shall pull through successfully. (VRE, 541)

7. THE EMPIRICAL IMPLICATIONS OF GOD'S EXISTENCE

1. This is a position he attributes primarily to the absolute idealists, but also to transcendentalists, stoics, and others (VRE, 374). James also labels this view "refined supernaturalism." He gives two names as well to his own position, "piecemeal supernaturalism" and "crass supernaturalism." James's use of the terms "crass" and "refined" supernaturalism, is meant to poke fun both at himself—here playing the role of the "Rocky Mountain tough"; as well as the false and pretentious refinement of the absolute idealists—here playing the role of the "Tender-minded Bostonian." See *Pragmatism,* Lecture I.

2. See also *Pragmatism* for a similar critique of absolute idealism:

> You cannot redescend into the world of particulars by the Absolute's aid, or deduce any necessary consequences of detail important for your life from your idea of his nature. He gives you indeed the assurance that all is well with *Him,*

and for his eternal way of thinking; but thereupon he leaves you to be finitely saved by your own temporal devices. (P, 40)

See "The Meaning of Truth" as well:

By escaping from your finite perceptions to the conception of the eternal whole, you can hallow any tendency whatever. Tho the absolute dictates nothing, it will sanction anything and everything after the fact, for whatever is once there will have to be regarded as an integral member of the universe's perfection. (MT, 123–24)

3. For more general statements of James's criteria of meaning which support this claim, see *Pragmatism,* Lecture II, and "Philosophical Conceptions and Practical Results," reprinted as Appendix I of *Pragmatism.*

4. See also James's suggestion that "all the special manifestations of religion may have been absurd (I mean its creeds and theories) . . ." (LWJ, 2:127).

5. It is interesting to note that A. J. Ayer, in his presentation of logical positivism in *Language, Truth and Logic* (London: V. Gollancz, 1936), was to arrive at a similar view of the philosopher's role. Unlike Ayer, James's conclusions are by no means positivistic.

6. Elsewhere in *Varieties* (397, 400), James offers other statements of what he takes to be the essence of religion, in which he approaches the question more from a psychological than a philosophical perspective.

7. Another obvious problem, as Rabbi Hayim Helevy Donin observes, is that frequently recited prayers, rather than being "service[s] of the heart," "may tend to deteriorate into routine recitations." (*To Be a Jew: A Guide to Jewish Observance in Contemporary Life* [New York: Basic Books, 1972], 160–61). By "routine recitations," Rabbi Donin has in mind behavior in which the subject "goes through the motions," without sincere spiritual engagement. These should be distinguished, of course, from other activities which may also be called "routine recitations," such as the continuous repetition

of a mantra, which causes the very disengagement from thought which is supposed to lead the subject into the desired spiritual state.

8. These particular forms of prayer are discussed in Richard Foster, *Prayer: Finding the Heart's True Home* (San Francisco: Harper San Franciso, 1992).

9. See VRE, Lectures IX, X, XVI, and XVII, especially 173–74, 197–98.

10. For the sake of clarity, whenever appropriate, in analyzing and assessing James's arguments, I shall substitute the terms "communion," "experience of communion," or "sense of communion" for James's use of the term "prayer."

11. Emphasis mine. James's emphasis removed.

12. Notice how James hedges in the following passage, to allow for a subjective interpretation of divine influence:

> Through prayer, religion insists, things which cannot be realized in any other manner come about: energy which but for prayer would be bound is by prayer set free and operates in some part, *be it objective or subjective,* of the world of facts. (VRE, 367, my emphasis; see also 376)

13. See also the following:

> [The subconscious region is] the larger part of each of us . . . the abode of everything that is latent and the reservoir of everything that passes unrecorded or unobserved. . . . Our intuitions, hypotheses, fancies, superstitions, persuasions, convictions, and in general all our non-rational operations come from it. It is the source of our dreams. . . . It is also the fountain-head of much that feeds our religion. In persons deep in the religious life . . . the door into this region seems unusually wide open. . . . (VRE, 381)

14. For an enlightening discussion of the differences between James's and Freud's views on the subconscious, see Myers, *William James,* 60, 377.

15. James's description of the experience of communion with the divine is strikingly similar to the description many in-

dividuals have given of their experience in the creative process. Perhaps the most prominent feature reported by individuals in their creative endeavors is the feeling that they are relying on some external power, or at least a power outside their own control. Creative insights appear more as gifts—visitations by "the Muse"—than the results of processes which individuals generate solely from within themselves. At the same time, the individual feels a strong sense of identification with the source of creative insight. Using the subconscious to explain creativity seems to account for both of these facts. (See Koestler, *The Act of Creation;* Ghiselin, *The Creative Process.*) James shows a certain cognizance of this fact. See VRE, 174, 188.

16. See also VRE, 411–12, 547. James's remarks on VRE, 192 n are also interesting as an indication of the degree to which he is treating his hypothesis as a scientific one.

17. Which in this passage he designates as "higher spiritual agencies."

18. This appears in a letter to Carl Stumpf, July 10, 1901. See also VRE, 550.

19. For other discussions of this position, see Fontinell, *Self, God, and Immortality;* Marcus Ford, *William James's Philosophy* (Amherst: University of Massachusetts Press, 1982); Levinson, *The Religious Investigations of William James.*

20. See especially Lectures I, VII, and VIII.

21. See also VRE, 161, 189; EPH, 157–59. For more on James's conception of God as an "indwelling divine," see PU, 18–19, PP, 2:315, 317.

22. Of particular relevance here is James's theory of pragmatic meaning, according to which a proposition must have predictive import in order to be pragmatically meaningful. As we have seen, James's claim in *Varieties* is that if a religious claim is to be meaningful, it must entail empirical consequences. In spite of this position, however, there are occasions, in both *Varieties* and *Pragmatism* (Lectures II and III), in which James is satisfied to count as sufficient for a religious claim being meaningful the fact that it entails future *metaphysical* consequences—for example, that after our deaths, our ideals ultimately will be preserved (VRE, 407). For further discussion of James's theory of meaning, see PPWJ, chapter 3.

23. The essay appears in James's *Essays in Religion and Morality.* John J. McDermott, in the "Introduction" to this volume, gives 1905 as the date for this essay (ERM, xix).

24. My emphases in first sentence. This passage is repeated, with a few small changes, in PU, 138.

25. See chapter 5, above.

26. See EPR, 134–36. See also SPP, 20, where James looks forward to the day when "science, metaphysics and religion may . . . form a single body of wisdom, and lend each other mutual support."

Bibliography of Works Cited

WORKS BY JAMES

All works by James except the *Letters,* are contained in *The Works of William James.* Edited by Frederick H. Burkhardt, Fredson Bowers, and Ignas K. Skrupskelis. Cambridge: Harvard University Press, 1975–1988. The original publication date appears in parentheses.

Essays in Philosophy, 1978.

Essays in Psychical Research, 1986.

Essays in Psychology, 1983.

Essays in Radical Empiricism, 1976 (1912).

Essays in Religion and Morality, 1982.

The Letters of William James. Edited by Henry James. 2 vols. Boston: The Atlantic Monthly Press, 1920.

Manuscript Lectures, 1988.

The Meaning of Truth, 1975 (1909).

Pragmatism, 1975 (1907).

The Principles of Psychology. 3 vols. 1981 (1890).

A Pluralistic Universe, 1977 (1909).

Some Problems of Philosophy, 1979 (1911).

Talks to Teachers on Psychology, and to Students on Some of Life's Ideals, 1983 (1899).

The Varieties of Religious Experience, 1985 (1902).

The Will to Believe, 1979 (1897).

WORKS BY OTHERS

Aristotle. *Nichomachean Ethics.* In *The Basic Works of Aristotle*, edited and with an introduction by Richard McKeon. New York: Random House, 1941.

Atkins, P. W. *The Periodic Kingdom.* New York: Basic Books, 1995.

Austin, J. L. "Performative-Constative." Translated by G. J. Warnock. In *Philosophy and Ordinary Language*, edited by Charles E. Caton. Urbana: University of Illinois Press, 1963.

Aveni, Anthony. *Conversing with the Planets: How Science and Myth Invented the Cosmos.* New York: Times Books, 1992.

Ayer, A. J. "Introduction" to *Pragmatism* and *The Meaning of Truth* by William James, vii–xxx. Cambridge: Harvard University Press, 1978.

———. *Language, Truth and Logic.* London: V. Gollancz, 1936.

———. *The Origins of Pragmatism.* San Francisco: Freeman, Cooper and Company, 1968.

Barbour, Ian. "Paradigms in Science and Religion." In *Paradigms and Revolutions*, edited by Gary Gutting. Notre Dame, Ind.: University of Notre Dame Press, 1980.

Bixler, Julius. *Religion in the Philosophy of William James.* Boston: Marshall Jones Company, 1926.

Blake, William. "Auguries of Innocence." In *The Norton Anthology of Poetry*, edited by Arthur M. Eastman et al. New York: W. W. Norton & Company, 1970.

Camus, Albert. "The Myth of Sisyphus." In *The Myth of Sisyphus and Other Essays*, translated by J. O'Brien. New York: Alfred A. Knopf, 1955.

Cavell, Stanley. *Must We Mean What We Say?* Cambridge: Cambridge University Press, 1969.

———. *The Senses of Walden: An Expanded Edition.* San Francisco: North Point Press, 1981.

Clebsch, William. *American Religious Thought: A History.* Chicago: University of Chicago Press, 1973.

Cooke, Deryck. *The Language of Music.* Oxford: Oxford University Press, 1959.

Copeland, Aaron. *Music and Imagination*. Cambridge: Harvard University Press, 1952.

Cotkin, George. *William James, Public Philosopher*. Baltimore: Johns Hopkins University Press, 1990.

"Dance." *New Yorker*, 30 July 1990, 5.

Donin, Hayim Helevy. *To Be a Jew: A Guide to Jewish Observance in Contemporary Life*. New York: Basic Books, 1972.

Durkheim, Emile. *The Elementary Forms of the Religious Life*. Translated by Joseph Ward Swain. London: George Allen and Unwin, 1957.

Einstein, Albert, et al. *Living Philosophies*. New York: Simon and Schuster, 1931.

Emerson, Ralph Waldo. *Essays* (First Series). Boston: Houghton, Mifflin and Company, 1904.

Feyerabend, Paul. *Against Method*. Rev. ed. London: Verso, 1988.

Feynman, Richard. *Surely You're Joking, Mr. Feynman!* New York: Bantam Books, 1986.

Finn, David. *Michelangelo's Three Pietàs: A Photographic Study*. Text by Frederick Hartt. New York: Harry N. Abrams, 1975.

Fontinell, Eugene. *Self, God and Immortality: A Jamesian Investigation*. Philadelphia: Temple University Press, 1986.

Ford, Marcus. *William James's Philosophy*. Amherst: University of Massachusetts Press, 1982.

Foster, Richard. *Prayer: Finding the Heart's True Home*. San Francisco: Harper San Franciso, 1992.

Freud, Sigmund. *The Future of an Illusion*. Translated by W. D. Robson-Scott. New York: Liveright Publishing Corporation, 1955.

———. *Letters of Sigmund Freud*. Edited by E. L. Freud. Translated by James Stern and Tania Stern. New York: Basic Books, 1960.

———. *Moses and Monotheism*. Translated by Katherine Jones. London: Hogarth Press, Ltd., 1951.

———. *Totem and Taboo*. Translated by A. A. Brill. New York: Moffat, Yard and Company, 1918.

Gavin, William Joseph. *William James and the Reinstatement of the Vague*. Philadelphia: Temple University Press, 1992.

Ghiselin, Brewster. *The Creative Process*. Berkeley: University of California Press, 1952.

Goldberg, Natalie. *Writing Down the Bones*. Boston: Shambhala Publications, 1986.

Goodman, Russell B. *American Philosophy and the Romantic Tradition*. Cambridge: Cambridge University Press, 1990.

Gotshalk, D. W. *Art and the Social Order*. Chicago: University of Chicago Press, 1947.

Hare, R. M. "Nothing Matters." In *Applications of Moral Philosophy*. Berkeley: University of California Press, 1972.

———. *Freedom and Reason*. New York: Oxford University Press, 1963.

———. *The Language of Morals*. New York: Oxford University Press, 1964.

Harman, Gilbert H. "Inference to the Best Explanation." *Philosophical Review* 74, no. 1 (January, 1965): 88–95.

Heilbrun, Carolyn. *Writing a Woman's Life*. New York: Ballantine Books, 1988.

Hempel, Carl. *Philosophy of Natural Science*. Englewood Cliffs, N.J.: Prentice Hall, 1966.

Heschel, Abraham Joshua. *The Insecurity of Freedom*. New York: Schocken Books, 1972.

Hesse, Mary. "Physics, Philosophy, and Myth." In *Physics, Philosophy and Theology: A Common Quest for Understanding*, edited by Robert J. Russell, William R. Stoeger, S.J., and George V. Coyne, S.J. Vatican City State: Vatican Observatory, 1988.

Hiley, David R., James F. Bohman, and Richard Shusterman, eds. *The Interpretive Turn*. Ithaca, N.Y.: Cornell University Press, 1991.

Hindemith, Paul. *The Craft of Musical Composition*. 4th ed. Translated by Arthur Mendel. London: Schott & Co., 1942.

Hollinger, David A. "The Problem of Pragmatism in American History." In *In The American Province*. Bloomington: Indiana University Press, 1985.

Holton, Gerald. *The Scientific Imagination: Case Studies*. Cambridge: Cambridge University Press, 1978.

Hopkins, Gerard Manley. "God's Grandeur." In *The Norton Anthology of Poetry*, edited by Arthur M. Eastman et al. New York: W. W. Norton & Company, 1970.

Hospers, John. *Meaning and Truth in the Arts.* Chapel Hill: University of North Carolina Press, 1946.

John Paul II. "Message of His Holiness Pope John Paul II." In *Physics, Philosophy and Theology: A Common Quest for Understanding*, edited by Robert J. Russell, William R. Stoeger, S.J., and George V. Coyne, S.J. Vatican City State: Vatican Observatory, 1988.

Johnson, Mark. *The Body in the Mind.* Chicago: University of Chicago Press, 1987.

Jones, Peter. "William James." In *American Philosophy*, edited by M. G. Singer. Cambridge: Cambridge University Press, 1985.

Katagiri, Dainin. *Returning to Silence.* Boston: Shambhala Publications, 1988.

Keller, Evelyn Fox. *A Feeling for the Organism.* New York: W.H. Freeman and Company, 1983.

Koestler, Arthur. *The Act of Creation.* London: Arkana Press, 1989.

Koyré, Alexandre. *The Astronomical Revolution.* New York: Dover Books, 1992.

Krishna, Daya. "Religious Experience, Language, and Truth." In *Religious Experience and Truth*, edited by Sidney Hook. New York: New York University Press, 1961.

Kuhn, Thomas. *The Structure of Scientific Revolutions.* 2d ed. Chicago: University of Chicago Press, 1970.

Lakoff, George, and Mark Johnson. *Metaphors We Live By.* Chicago: University of Chicago Press, 1980.

le Huray, Peter, and James Day, eds. *Music and Aesthetics in the Eighteenth and Early-Nineteenth Centuries.* Cambridge: Cambridge University Press, 1981.

Leuba, James H. "Professor William James' Interpretation of Religious Experience." *International Journal of Ethics* 14 (April, 1904): 322–39.

Levinson, Henry Samuel. *The Religious Investigations of William James.* Chapel Hill: University of North Carolina Press, 1981.

Lewis, C. S. *Mere Christianity*. New York: Macmillan Publishing Company, 1943.

Lipton, Peter. *Inference to the Best Explanation*. London: Routledge, 1991.

Mackie, J. L. *The Miracle of Theism*. Oxford: Oxford University Press, 1982.

McDermott, John J. "Feeling as Insight: The Affective Dimension of Social Diagnosis." In *The Culture of Experience: Philosophical Essays in the American Grain*. New York: New York University Press, 1976.

————. "Introduction" to *Essays in Religion and Morality* by William James. Cambridge: Harvard University Press, 1982.

McNulty, Faith. "Review of A. N. Wilson, *C. S. Lewis*." *New Yorker*, 26 November 1990, 130–44.

Mehta, Ved. *Mahatma Gandhi and His Apostles*. New York: Penguin Books, 1977.

Merton, Thomas. *The Seven Storey Mountain*. New York: Harcourt Brace Jovanovich, 1948.

————. *The Sign of Jonas*. New York: Harcourt Brace Jovanovich, 1953.

Mill, John Stuart. *Utilitarianism*. Edited by Samuel Gorovitz. New York: The Bobbs Merrill Company, 1971.

Miller, Dickinson. "'The Will to Believe' and the Duty to Doubt." *International Journal of Ethics* 9 (1898–99): 169–95.

Monk, Ray. *Wittgenstein: The Duty of Genius*. New York: Macmillan Publishing Company, 1990.

Munsterberg, Hugo. *The Crown of Life: Artistic Creativity in Old Age*. San Diego: Harcourt Brace Jovanovich, 1983.

Myers, Gerald E. *William James*. New Haven: Yale University Press, 1986.

Nagel, Thomas. "The Absurd." *Journal of Philosophy* 68, no. 20 (October 21, 1971): 716–27.

Nakhnikian, George. "On the Cognitive Import of Certain Conscious States." In *Religious Experience and Truth*, edited by Sidney Hook. New York: New York University Press, 1961.

Otto, Rudolph. *The Idea of the Holy*. Oxford: Oxford University Press, 1923.

Passmore, John. *Serious Art.* London: Duckworth, 1991.

Peirce, C. S. "The Fixation of Belief." In *The Collected Papers of Charles Sanders Peirce,* vol. 5, edited by Charles Hartshorne and Paul Weiss. Cambridge: Harvard University Press, 1934.

Perkins, Moreland. "Notes on the Pragmatic Theory of Truth." *The Journal of Philosophy* 49, no. 18 (August 28, 1952): 573–87.

Perry, Ralph Barton. *In The Spirit of William James.* Bloomington: Indiana University Press, 1958.

———. *The Thought and Character of William James.* 2 vols. Boston: Little, Brown and Company, 1935.

Plantinga, Alvin. "Reason and Belief in God." In *Faith and Rationality: Reason and Belief in God,* edited by Alvin Plantinga and Nicholas Wolterstorff. Notre Dame, Ind.: University of Notre Dame Press, 1983.

Putnam, Hilary. *Reason, Truth and History.* Cambridge: Cambridge University Press, 1981.

———. *The Many Faces of Realism.* La Salle, Ill.: Open Court Publishing Company, 1987.

Quine, W. V. O. Essay (untitled). In *What I Believe,* edited by Mark Booth. New York: Crossroad Publishing Company, 1984.

Ramsey, Bennett. *Submitting to Freedom: The Religious Vision of William James.* Oxford: Oxford University Press, 1993.

Reichenbach, Hans. *Experience and Prediction.* Chicago: University of Chicago Press, 1938.

Reik, Theodor. *The Haunting Melody.* New York: Farrar, Straus and Young, 1953.

Renan, Ernest. *Drames Philosophiques.* Paris: Calmann-Levy, 1888.

Russell, Bertrand. "William James's Conception of Truth." In *Philosophical Essays.* New York: Simon and Schuster, 1968.

———. *Religion and Science.* Oxford: Oxford University Press, 1961.

———. *Why I Am Not A Christian.* New York: George Allen and Unwin, 1957.

Sacks, Oliver. "An Anthropologist on Mars." In *An Anthropologist on Mars: Seven Paradoxical Tales.* New York: Alfred A. Knopf, 1995.

Santayana, George. "William James." In *Character and Opinion in the United States.* New York: Charles Scribner's Sons, 1920.

Schleiermacher, Friedrich. *Soliloquies.* Translated by Horace Leland Friess. Chicago: Open Court Publishing Company, 1957.

Schopenhauer, Arthur. *The World as Will and Idea.* 3 vols. London: Routledge and Kegan Paul, 1957.

Seigfried, Charlene Haddock. *William James's Radical Reconstruction of Philosophy.* Albany: State University of New York Press, 1990.

Smart, Ninian. *The Philosophy Of Religion.* New York: Oxford University Press, 1979.

Smith, John E. "Introduction" to *The Varieties of Religious Experience* by William James, xi–li. Cambridge: Harvard University Press, 1985.

Solomon, Robert. "The Virtue of Love." *Midwest Studies in Philosophy,* vol. 13. Notre Dame, Ind.: University of Notre Dame Press, 1988.

Sonneck, O. G., ed. *Beethoven: Impressions by His Contemporaries.* New York: Dover Publications, 1967.

Suckiel, Ellen Kappy. *The Pragmatic Philosophy of William James.* Notre Dame, Ind.: University of Notre Dame Press, 1982.

Sullivan, J. W. N. *Beethoven: His Spiritual Development.* New York: Vintage Books, 1960.

Thayer, HS. "Introduction" to *Pragmatism* by William James, xi–xxxviii. Cambridge: Harvard University Press, 1975.

Updike, John. "Forward" to *The Complete Stories* by Franz Kafka. New York: Schocken Books, 1971.

Vaughan Williams, Ralph. "What is Music?" In *National Music and Other Essays.* Oxford: Oxford University Press, 1987.

Viladesau, Richard. "Music as an Approach to God: A Theology of Aesthetic Experience." *Catholic World* 232, no. 1387 (January/February, 1989): 4–9.

The Way of A Pilgrim, published with *The Pilgrim Continues His Way*. Translated by R. M. French. San Francisco: Harper San Francisco, 1973.

Weil, Simone. *Waiting for God*. New York: G. P. Putnam's Sons, 1951.

Wiesel, Elie. *Souls on Fire: Portraits and Legends of Hasidic Masters*. New York: Summit Books, 1972.

Williams, Bernard. *Morality*. New York: Harper and Row, 1972.

Wilson, A. N. *C. S. Lewis*. New York: W. W. Norton & Company, 1990.

Wittgenstein, Ludwig. *Ludwig Wittgenstein, Letters To Russell, Keynes and Moore*. Edited by G. H. von Wright. Ithaca, N.Y.: Cornell University Press, 1974.

Zeki, Semir, "The Visual Image in Mind and Brain." *Scientific American* 267, no. 3 (September, 1992): 68–76.

Index

Abauzit, Frank, 136
Aberkains, Sandra, 146
Absolute, the, 81
adaptation, 99–101
agnosticism, 7, 12, 29
Anscombe, Elizabeth, 133–34
Aquinas, Thomas, 48
Aristotle, 141, 153
Arnim, Bettina von, 149
astronomy, 157
atheism, 29
Austin, John, 159
autism, 73–74
Aveni, Anthony, 157
Ayer, A. J., 81–82, 88, 90,
    136, 163

Baal Shem Tov, Israel, 145
Barbour, Ian, 87
Beethoven, Ludwig von, 26,
    50–51, 143, 149
belief, religious: empirical
    confirmation of, 14, 93,
    113–31; genesis of, 8–9;
    inferior varieties of, 102, 159;
    James's personal, 4;
    justification of, 5–8, 12–14,
    27–56, 71–73, 75, 88–89,
    92–93, 97–113, 127, 161

(see also interpretation); as
    justified in the context of
    emotional investment, 33–37;
    as mankind's most important
    function, 105–6; and moral
    commitment, 101; moral
    implications of, 104–6,
    109–12 (see also perfection,
    moral); normative element of,
    158; personal nature of, 6, 8,
    11, 80, 94, 117, 127; and
    self-interest, 97–100
Bixler, Julius, 159
Black, Max, 48
Blake, William, 21
Buddhism, 138

Calvin, John, 134
Camus, Albert, 18
categorical imperative, 24
Cavell, Stanley, 154
charity, excess of, 102
Chautauqua, 108–9
Christianity, 10, 35, 58; ideals
    of, 110; James's attitude
    toward, 5, 133
claims, religious, pragmatic
    meaning of, 34–36, 129. See
    also belief, religious; discourse

177

About the Author

Ellen Kappy Suckiel is Professor of Philosophy at the University of California, Santa Cruz, and the author of *The Pragmatic Philosophy of William James* (Notre Dame Press, 1982).